CW00871687

meta-synthesis

Orange Gate Journal

A Personal View of the
Greenham Common Women's Peace Camp

Ginette Leach

To Chris,
with very best wishes for

Ginette

Orange Gate Journal

A Personal View of the
Greenham Common Women's Peace Camp

Ginette Leach

meta-synthesis

Copyright © (text) Ginette Leach

Copyright © (front cover, The Eviction of Sally & back cover, Orange Gate & insert of Ginette Typing at Orange Gate) Mark Leach

All rights reserved. This book or any portion thereof may not be reproduced or used in any manner whatsoever without the express written permission of the publisher except for the use of brief quotations in a book review or scholarly journal.

First Printing: 2014

ISBN 978-1-312-71742-8

Meta-Synthesis
56 Downland Road
Woodingdean
Brighton
BN2 6DJ
UK

www.meta-synthesis.com

Ordering Information:

Special discounts are available on quantity purchases by corporations, associations, educators, and others. For details, contact the publisher at the above listed address, or email:

mark@meta-synthesis.com

To

Greenham Women Everywhere

Foreword

From November 1982 until January 1985, Ginette was a visitor and then a regular member of the women's community at Orange Gate, part of the Greenham Common Women's Peace Camp. Orange was one of seven gates into RAF Greenham Common. All the gates had women's peace camps that infuriated officialdom.

American [USAF] cruise missile nuclear weapons were deployed at Greenham Common in 1983.

Ginette's personal – and often very funny – perspective was written within hours of it happening. This book is a very lightly edited and reformatted version of the original document. A few of the identifying names have been changed.

While the early 1980s may seem rather recent history to many of us: in 1984 there were no mobile phones, there was no M25 orbital motorway bypassing London and the Cold War seemed as if it would **heat up** *at a moment's notice.*

The original typed manuscript, plus a couple of artefacts – including the portable typewriter used by Ginette and the set of bolt cutters provided by the Betteshanger Colliery miners – have been donated to the Women's Library at the London School of Economics (LSE).

Scans of the original typed manuscript [PDF] are available for view at:

> **www.orangegatejournal.co.uk**

The Orange Gate Journal website has been archived for preservation by the British Library:

> **www.webarchive.org.uk/ukwa/target/64290919/collection/ 98537/source/collection**

Ginette's journal and life were dramatised in December 2014, as part of the BBC Radio 4 *Writing The Century* series. Five 12-minute episodes were broadcast over one week in the Women's Hour 10:45am drama slot, repeated later in the evening at 7:45pm.

Glossary of Terms, Some People & Places

ABH	Actual Bodily Harm
Aldermaston	Atomic Weapons Research Establishment (10 miles east of Greenham)
Base	RAF Greenham Common, housing USAF Cruise Missiles
Bruce Kent	CND Chairperson and a national figure in 1984
Burghfield	UK Atomic Weapon Factory (20 miles away)
Caroline Blackwood	Author & journalist (1931 – 1996)
CND	Campaign for Nuclear Disarmament
Deal	East Kent town where Ginette lived
Faslane	UK Nuclear Submarine base in Scotland
GBH	Grievous Bodily Harm
Hotties	Hot water bottles
Jill Tweedie	Feminist, writer and Guardian Journalist, who had a house in Deal (1936 – 1993)
Joan Ruddock	CND Chair. Later became an MP then an MEP
Kenny Lynch	Entertainer/personality from the 1960s
MoD	Ministry of Defence
NATO	North Atlantic Treaty Organisation
NVDA	Non-Violent Direct Action
Pat Arrowsmith	Peace Activist and Co-founder of CND
The Van	Peter Darlington Peace Van
SWP	Socialist Workers Party
USAF	United States Air Force
WPC	Woman Police Constable
WVS	Women's Voluntary Service

The Seven Gates (Names did change)

Blue	Gate nearest to Newbury train station
Green	Secluded camp in woods
Orange	Ginette's Gate, at the eastern end of the base
Red	Smaller camp on grass verge
Turquoise	Not always occupied
Violet/Indigo	Benders other side of the road
Yellow	Main Gate and the original Peace Camp

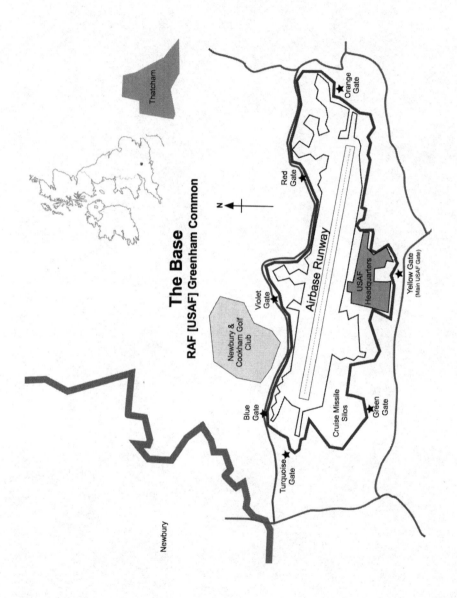

The Base
RAF [USAF] Greenham Common

Thatcham

N

Newbury

Newbury & Cookham Golf Club

Blue Gate

Turquoise Gate

Violet Gate

Red Gate

Orange Gate

Airbase Runway

USAF Headquarters

Yellow Gate
(Main USAF Gate)

Green Gate

Cruise Missile Silos

November 1982

We got to Greenham Common about fifteen minutes late, as we were directed the wrong way by a non-local policeman controlling Newbury race day traffic. We saw the vast mesh fence, with outward facing strands of barbed wire on top, and thought we must come to the main entrance soon. Inside the wire was short grass, buildings every now and then, many obviously not in use with broken windows and a neglected appearance. Others were neatly painted, drab, and rather ominous. Then there were odd pipes and what looked almost like chimney pots sticking out of the ground, with huge notices on the perimeter fence, warning *'No naked flames beyond this point'*. The narrow road followed the fence for miles (later we learned 9 miles), but really there was nothing to see. The contrast between the stark camp on one side, and on the other, the rough heather, clumpy grass, bracken and trees, with a golf club, two private schools, one for boys, one for girls, large private houses, small farms, all typical, pretty English countryside, was overpowering. Once or twice we lost the high fence, but kept turning right, and soon came back to it again. We did not see a runway, planes, people or anything tangible, just the short, tidy, undulating grass. We could rarely see inside more than a hundred yards or so, sometimes much less.

Eventually we turned right again onto a much busier main road. Soon, on the left, pulled onto the common amongst the trees and shrubs, we saw the Peace Van, various piles of things in plastic bags, and bedding hung on bushes to dry in the October sunshine. I pulled in next to the van and when we got out and looked across the road, we saw huge piles of granite that had been dumped by the authorities to stop the women camping on the grass verges on each side of the drive leading to the entrance. Over on the left people were just quietly wandering around, and leading their own lives. We looked in the van, which had untidy piles or bedding, clothing etc., all over the place, and was still obviously being lived in. The back doors were wide open, to dry out the interior.

We walked across the road, and looked at the peace signs painted in letters all over the granite blocks. The smaller stones were arranged in CND symbols, and there was string in a cat's cradle sort of arrangement in a couple of places. (The women had done the string thing only the night before as we were told they like to do something different every Friday night.) By this time, our presence was noticed and a couple of the women came towards us. We explained we had come for the Van. Norman showed them the letter he had received from Newbury Council saying that the Van would be removed forthwith as parking was not permitted on common. They were not particularly perturbed, just glad that they had had the use of it, and remarked that the battery was flat and they had not finished clearing it out. By now we had reached their actual campsite, which was on a small piece of ground just to the left of the entrance, almost next to the guard who controlled the huge gates, right up against the fence.

I must explain this is not like a campsite where you have a pleasant two weeks holiday in the sun by the sea. The authorities allow no vehicles or tents. Therefore, there is no privacy or protection from the weather. The materials most in evidence are mud, granite blocks and stones, and most of all polythene and plastic. In some ways, it is rather like the worst type of gypsy encampment, but it is not. It is permanent organised chaos. The campfire was burning briskly, and round it were women sitting on stones, chatting quietly, eating a flan and drinking tea or coffee. Blackened pots, pans etc., were hung up neatly on nails on a board, and there were other boards and tables covered with food and utensils. One plastic dustbin was labelled 'plates' and another 'veg', and round the campfire granite stones had been packed into the mud to a kind of rough drying walking and sitting area. Women were preparing food, peeling potatoes, washing up, just wandering around, or sitting quietly. Two children were playing on a patch of grass with a coloured ball. The whole place had an air of quietness and almost lethargy. We realised that when we said we would arrive at 4pm and were twenty minutes late, nobody had noticed, because time meant absolutely nothing to them. They looked fit, well and clean. Well-washed hands and faces, clean, tidy hair, and trousers, sweaters and various types of boots were certainly no dirtier or scruffier than our own. The children were pink-cheeked and obviously healthy, and we were told that they had adapted to the life well.

All around the camp were piles and piles of plastic bags, covered with rather muddy layers of multi-coloured polythene sheets. When we were looking for a missing tent and trying to sort through those piles of bags, gradually the wet in and round them from days of rain, seeped, dripped, and then ran down through the piles, round our feet. Everything was damp, some things soaking, but this was just accepted by the women as part of their lives. They told us when the rain was at its heaviest, someone provided huge umbrellas and they just sat under them round the campfire for hours on end.

After a while, two women came to the Peace Van with us to help clear it out. Luckily, I had some jump leads in my car so it started OK and we took it over the road, up the drive, along a short narrow, muddy track, where there three old VW dormobile-type vans were parked. We took some time to unload the Peace Van: blankets, clothes, food crockery, one old cider bottle, bits and pieces of rubbish, etc., etc. We put as much as we could into one of the already completely full dormobiles, which was so packed, I could not get inside it. I asked one woman where everyone slept, and she vaguely pointed to the vans and said, "Two here, two there and two more there with the children, and the rest under polythene in the main camp by the gate." As there were at any one time between 12 and 20 women, it seemed quite ludicrous, but again as with answers to any questions, all was low key, just a slight shrug and a feeling that nothing was impossible, they managed, coped.

Another strangeness I found was while this hard but peaceful life was going on outside the gates, these gates themselves were being constantly opened and closed for the Base traffic. Large cars with American number plates, vans, general noise, bustle and men. Both parties pretty well ignored each other, but as an outsider, I was very aware of the internal activity. The sound of a bugle being blown inside, while outside three or four woman had come back to the camp carrying a marvellous Chinese lantern, which there were trying to string up rather ineffectively on some poles. When Norman and I parked our vehicles on the entrance road, straight away I was asked by the guard to move mine. I said I would and then took some more pictures of the camp before doing so. I knew I was no real threat to them, just a visitor, and although someone probably took note of my car registration number, and perhaps photos of Norman and myself for the files, we were no more than a slight irritation. Actually when we did try to go, the van would not start again and to get my car battery near to the van's, I pulled right across the road blocking it completely, and nobody said a thing.

As to the women themselves? Well, this is not easy. They were all young, in their twenties and thirties, except for an older one who had arrived that day from Derbyshire, and a couple of teenagers. They had been there for varying times; one in her early twenties with punk yellow hair, who had been there over six months, was obviously rather extrovert and friendly. Others were quiet, ordinary young women, hard to describe, just nice, but very dedicated. Mind you, they would have to be to live at Greenham Common. I wonder what their families think of them? Somehow I felt I wanted to organise them better. Sort out those piles of 'things' lying around and chuck out the useless stuff. Get word round to peace groups, CND members and all who want to help, and say that they need money to buy the things *they* want, not food or clothes that they don't really need. I don't think the authorities that try to move them on really realise what they are up against. These women will not be moved. I asked one (actually I felt a fool as soon as I had), what will happen next? She looked surprised and said of course they would stay, nothing would happen, nothing could happen. Their faith in themselves, in the closed community that they have created, almost shut out outsiders like Norman and me. They were polite and friendly to us, helpful in finding mugs and plates from the Peace Van, but we were not even a diversion as far as they were concerned. We weren't offered a cup of anything, although we told them we had driven 150 miles there and were going straight back. They thanked us for the use of the Van, but were not that upset that it was going. They would manage. Only three of them talked to us, the others just smiled politely. Obviously, friendships and loves are very strong there, there is no way one could be alone. It is a community of like-minded women as dedicated as they are, or quit within a few days. I think I would like to join them, but on second thoughts I know I am not strong enough in body (I like my creature comforts) or spirit (I am not totally sure they are doing the right thing for peace), to live as they do.

12th – 13th December 1982

We left Deal in the Peace Van at about 7.45am and made good time to Thatcham where the rendezvous was to take place. We drove round the village until we were sure our coach was not there, then stopped and made coffee. Eventually it arrived and followed us the last few miles to Newbury and Greenham Common Air Base. This took an hour or so, as the roads were totally jammed with coaches and cars all covered in anti-nuclear stickers. There was a great feeling of relief that we were not the only ones to have come on this day, and I think everyone felt this, as there was a lot of talking between vehicles, with drivers and passengers wanting to know where we were from and about the Peace Van itself. By this time, we were joined by hundreds walking to the Base, so before long we pulled on to the side of the road and walked to Gate 8. The whole drive had been in rain varying from drizzle, bucketing, to sleet. However, as we reached Greenham it cleared and I saw no more rain.

Norman had prepared 8 gallons of soup for the women, so he took the Van off to Gate 7 where it was needed. In small groups, we wandered round the perimeter fence trying to find room among the women already there, to link arms and tie our personal mementoes to the fence. There was a great air of friendliness, goodwill and peace, (this is what Christmas should be like!), everyone talking and saying that if they moved up a little there was room for us with them. Coffee and sandwiches were passed round, and the mud underfoot was forgotten. Some women were singing, and the songs got passed on down the line. As the fence is 9 miles long, and it was completely surrounded, sometimes with women two or three deep, I'm not sure how the estimate of 30,000 was obtained. I never saw more than a few hundred at a time, although at one point as we came up a rise and looked across the bleak short cut grass of the Base, there was the fence in the distance, and a mass of women behind it. Again the feeling of solidarity, it was not just us where we were, we really were surrounding the Base.

Elizabeth's bag with the nappies had been left by mistake in the Peace Van, so a few of us strolled through the mud to find it, meeting friends from Canterbury and other places on the way. Norman was doing a fantastic trade in soup. He was giving it free, but saying that any donations would go to the Women at Greenham Peace Camp. He and his son Robert worked for hours, taking £44.85 in donations.

They were much too busy to stop and talk, so I went off to see if anyone could advise me where to park the Peace Van for the night. The only advice I got was to choose a spot and stay there. Masses of tiny tents were already being erected, as well as a few much larger ones, which were sort of information places, but the organisation was so low key that really, you could just please yourself and be welcome anywhere. I felt very responsible not only for the Peace Van, but also for the four others, Hilary, and Pam, Rose and Bev from Dover who were staying the night in the van.

By this time it was getting dark and all-round the fence candles were lit and left stuck in the ground at the foot of the fence. We felt it was time to be heading back to the coach that was a couple of miles away. I arranged with Hilary that we would meet at Gate 7 where Norman had been serving soup. We walked slowly round the fence, but when we got back to the main road we realised there was no way Norman would be able to drive the Van down and turn it over to me, so I walked back, to find him clearing everything up. To cut a long story short, eventually he, Robert and I drove back to as near the coach as we could, then they left and I took over the van. Fine, all I had to do was retrace our steps. The trouble was, apart from the road being jammed with walkers, the police would not let me turn up the correct road, and I was directed to Thatcham, Newbury, and then the village of Greenham. I was assured that the road I wanted was completely blocked by cars, (this was a complete lie, it was empty), so I had to do this huge circle round. When I finally reached the perimeter fence at Gate 4, I had to persuade a friendly copper to let me drive against the flow of traffic down my road. By this time it was totally dark apart from candles, torches and campfires at Gates 5 and 6, both of which were crowded with women plus a few policemen.

At last, I got to Gate 7 but there was no sign of Hilary or the others, so I parked and opened a bottle of wine with the help of a friendly policeman, who accepted a quick slurp for his efforts (when his colleagues were not looking). I set off peering at faces and calling "Hilary", "Pam", "Rose", "Bev", and asking various women if they had seen the crowd from Deal and Dover. I decided to walk on down the hill a bit in case we had out wires crossed. It was very strange, quiet and spooky, but the candles shone brightly in the absolutely still air, so that on the fence the peace symbols, pictures, banners, spiders webs of wool, toys, clothes, ribbons, grass woven into words, photos, balloons, and messages, could all be seen, but the mud and Base itself were hidden.

We all met up eventually in the right place, drank our wine, had some food and went to the main tent to make plans for the morning. It was all a bit of a muddle and low key, so although we were very welcome to stay with them and their 5am start, they felt we might be of more use at Gate 8 where there was more organisation. So we went there, found the right tent, were given various instructions as to briefings and signing on in the morning before 9, and told that we should talk out among ourselves who was prepared to be arrested, and who to be legal observer and driver. The ideal number for a group was 10, but there would be more to join our group. We went back to the Van, had another drink, sat, talked and read the information carefully. We soon agreed what each individual within the group should do, and got into our sleeping bags.

I do not think any of us got much sleep, but at least we were dry and apart from the two in the back of the Van, warm. I found it hard to switch off, so many sights and people. Someone earlier had remarked that they had no idea there were "so many dropout, unemployed, lesbian, commie women in England"!

The next morning we roused ourselves at about 6.45. Getting up had to be in strict rotation, so Pam was the worker and I was last up. After coffee, I decided it was time I tried the loos rather than a very skimpy leafless bramble bush beside the main road. On the way there, I passed Gate 8 where about ten women had been since 6am. They looked very cold indeed, one particularly who had gone very white and said she felt sick. The others persuaded her to go and get warm, and when I offered tea, they said they really needed it. On the way back to the Van, which was quite a way, I met Julien, a lad whom I had seen the previous week at a vigil outside Canterbury prison in support of Gus Hutchinson. Gus, like the Greenham Common women, had been sent there for 14 days for refusing to pay his fine for obstructing vehicles at Molesworth Air Base. Julien was in quite a state having hitched to Greenham the evening before. I don't think he'd realised this was a women's demo and he told some tale about losing his sleeping bag, so he'd spent the night sitting by a camp fire. I took him back to the Peace Van to thaw out, gave him a vast breakfast, which stopped him shaking and looking blue, while Pam made up flasks of tea. Hilary and I took these back to the grateful women on Gate 8.

As soon as we got back, we all went to the information tent. Inside we squatted on muddy straw and were soon joined by a woman from Leeds called Wendy, two Londoners and two Quakers from Birmingham. This was an ideal number and we called ourselves the Peter Darlington Group. Our instructor asked us a few questions about what we were prepared to do, and told us how to go limp when arrested and various other encouraging things at 8.30 on a cold damp Monday morning. At that moment, the BBC TV camera crew came in to film us, and a short excerpt was shown on the box that night. (Isn't it odd how the people you don't want to see you, *do*, and those you do want to, *you don't?*)

We finished our briefing and were leaving when an urgent call on the walkie-talkie asked for more women to go to Gap E. In the perimeter fence, there are eight official gates, but apart from these, there are five gaps, where the internal roads on the base come to the fence, and the overhanging barbed wire can be unwound, the chain link plastic covered fencing unbolted from a concrete post, the two posts alongside it pulled up, and there you have extra exits. The Greenham Common Women knew that if these gaps were left unguarded they would be an excellent way to get the American personnel in and out. We set off to Gap E in the Peace Van, but as suspected found the police wouldn't let me drive up the right road, so everyone piled out and I took the van back to Gate 8, and followed the others on foot. By the time I arrived, it was about a mile away, there were 50 or 60 women there, sitting and standing round the fence. We decided we would also make a roadblock to stop the police passing in their vehicles, so some plastic sheeting was put on the ground and women sat on it to block the road completely. This was our rather negative task for the day, but many incidents took place, and although it was pretty chilly waiting from about 10 to 3.30, I hardly felt the cold.

About every hour, a Land Rover came down the internal road, stopped for a few minutes, and two military policeman had, I guess, a rough head count. The country road was much busier. The police obviously had to let the local people through, so varying from sympathy to hatred, vehicles were driven up to the seated women, who got up, pulled back enough plastic sheeting for the vehicle to pass, then put it back and saw down again. We were novices at this game, and got badly caught out early on, when a woman came tearing down to us, yelling that she was urgently taking her child to hospital and we must let her through instantly. Of course we did so, and just as she was starting to pass us, three police cars tore after her, so close that there was no way we could prevent them coming through inches behind her. We were all furious so after that some of us stood a few yards up the road, slowing vehicles and checking identities. That, in itself, could be pretty unpleasant, as I tried to stop one car and he just came on at me. I held my ground (actually, I was quite mesmerised) and eventually he screamed to a halt not more than six inches away from my legs. Early on many of the cars were for the Press, but after a while the police banned them, so they had to hump cameras etc. up the hill on foot.

We were able to hear what was happening in other areas as every Gate and Gap had a walkie-talkie. We heard that there was trouble at Gate 4 where arrests had been made, so we held an impromptu meeting to decide whether we should help them or stay where we were. A few went to help, but as it was about 3 miles away, most of us felt that we could do more good by not making Gap E too vulnerable. It wasn't an easy decision for our group, but I think we were right.

Police cars would often be seen on our road, and at once we all positioned ourselves so they had to turn round and go back. Once two policemen walked up and although we were right across they pushed and shoved until they got through, and there was nothing we could do about it. Perhaps we should have tried ourselves together with string, but one always think of things like that too late. Many foreign as well as British reporters passed us, many stopped and talked, but we did not see the much-publicised Russians. We were a bit irritated by the private plane that flew round and round with a banner declaring "*Kremlin Sends Congratulations*", but somehow it was irrelevant and not worth bothering about.

All day at our Gap we had three Buddhist women in their saffron robes beating and chanting a steady rhythm. Their inner strength and dedication was remarkable and they hardly stirred all day. The only time they moved was when they had some food, and for a few minutes then they walked around to stretch their legs.

At 12.55 there was a co-ordinated 5-minute silent vigil round the whole Base. Soon after, we had another meeting. It appeared that someone had suggested that we ought to make a gesture by pulling back the fence at the Gap going inside it was rather useless doing this just at Gap E, and it ought to be done at all the Gates and Gaps. Most of the other groups were in agreement.

By then it was about 2 o'clock, and as we had masses of food back in the Van, I volunteered to go back and get some, and Bev came with me. We made three flasks of coffee and took all the food we could carry back with us. Hilary greeted us with the news that some of the women had gone inside the fence after all, and there was evidence glowing brighter as darkness fell, two candles burning away. I was glad they had gone inside, but sorry I missed being there to witness, and probably participate.

The women were starting to drift off by this time, so once the coffee was finished, we decided to go back to the Van. It was getting very cold now, and we had a long way to go, but not nearly so far as some. Edinburgh, Cornwall, Wales, Leeds, the Midlands, even a group from Dublin, so Deal and Dover did not seem so bad.

I heated up some soup while the others went off to the loos. Soon Hilary came back and said that they all wanted to stay until 6 when the women would leave the Gates. I agreed, and we took the last bottle of wine back to the others. There was a big campfire burning, the bottle was passed round. We sang and danced and yelled, all linking arms and behaving like schoolgirls on the last day of term. There must have been about 70 of us, shouting, whooping, praying, doing our own thing, and the few police and men who were clearing up the camping area, looked surprised and were perhaps a little envious. Men do not behave like that. Women don't often, either, but these two days had been *our* days.

Eventually we went back to the van, had our soup, met up with Carolyn from Canterbury who wanted a lift, and set off for home just before 7pm. It was a very long drive, and I think the others enjoyed their sleep; I got back at 11, but although I was exhausted, couldn't get to sleep for ages.

On that drive and since I have had plenty of time to think about those two days. The media have given it a lot of coverage, but the impressions and feelings will last a long time for those who were actually there. The main thing was: *it worked*. 30,000 women did turn up, and with very little organisation they all put mementoes on the fence, lit candles, talked, and shared ideas, food, drink and the experience. When we arrived it all seemed chaos and muddle, but we sorted ourselves without the aid of a single steward. The strident banners and slogans and newspaper selling and leaflets about other rallies were out of place at Greenham, and the few men with these quickly faded away. On the Monday when we asked what should we do, it was always *suggested*, but it was up to us as a small group to carry out that suggestion, or not, as we felt. We were in this together: the meetings in the middle of the road, the shared fear of speeding cars and the police, the argument with the military officer who was not let down our road even after he took off his uniform jacket, the soggy bit of field - through the barbed wire fence over the road - where everyone had to go for a pee. The only way to describe both the good and the bad is solidarity and a greater strength to stop cruise missiles and all nuclear weapons from being based in this country, and the Women of Greenham Common Peace Camp led the way.

Easter 1983

We went to Burghfield this time, as we were a mixed party of eight, Mike, Hilary, Robert, Peter, Sue, Konrad, Richard and myself. We made careful preparations and all attended the NVDA day to get to know each other better, and to become a group rather than individuals. This was important and I think we had a rougher time there with Paul and his '*police*' tactics than we did on the actual blockading. Then the group had another meeting to work out finances, logistics, tents, food, drink, etc. We all put money in the kitty for food and Hilary and Richard did the buying. Sue made a quiche for the first evening and Hilary a rice loaf for the second. I think our only slight mistake was too much bread and not enough orange juice, but the catering was fantastic. Other CND members from Deal gave us cakes and extra eggs. Paul made out cards with his phone number and address for contact in case we were arrested, as by now we had decided who was prepared for arrest and who was to observe. This planning was all necessary and it worked without a hitch.

Sue picked me up soon after 3 o'clock on Wednesday afternoon and we collected Robert. Peter had decided to go on his motorbike but even so, the car was pretty full. We arrived at the Burghfield camp site soon after 6.30, met Peter, and I put my small tent up near the Canterbury group, leaving enough room for our six man tent, as the site was rapidly filling, and getting muddier. There were two large marquee tents for the organisers, roped off paths, a sort of DIY loo and pit area, people directing traffic. In fact, the whole place was starting to buzz. By 8.45, we were getting worried. The Peace Van had not arrived, yet it had left Deal about the same time as we did. Just as Sue and Peter were going to phone Paul to check, it arrived, and we were able to park it quite close to the tents where it was to be used as a communication centre. (In the event it was hardly used officially, so we were lucky enough to use it ourselves). We put up the big tent, went and saw the organisers about the roster for the next day, had a huge supper and wine, and then went for our official workshop and briefing. By the time we crawled back to our tents it was nearly 2am, and we had to be up by 4.45 to go to the Daffodil Gate by 6am. The lucky ones had a little sleep! We had been a bit worried about getting up in time, but men with megaphones boomed at us ay a quarter to five so we had no excuse for staying in our comparatively warm sleeping bags any longer. My son, Mark, had joined me from Salford the previous evening, and was on a later shift, so I piled my sleeping bags on to him and met the Deal people outside the tent in the cold, damp darkness.

There were hundreds of people milling about, so our two observers collected some food, we made sure the phone number we had written on our arms the night before had not rubbed off, and set off with a big bunch to the Daffodil Gate. There are three gates at Burghfield, called by CND, Daffodil, Tulip and Bluebell, and we went off at a spanking pace. After about half an hour, we arrived at a gate, but the wrong one! It was Tulip, so we carried on round the factory fence and road an eventually after walking for over an hour in total, got to the right gate and joined the other demonstrators, press and police. There must have been about 30 demonstrators, nearly as many TV crews and press, including some from the States and Canada, and quite a lot of police lined up, with reinforcements sitting in vans just along the road.

Blockading is never as simple as it sounds. Vehicles can be stopped unless one is physically moved, but pedestrians and local residents are not so easy. There was a walkie-talkie to keep in touch with other gates, and our main task was to stop workers either entering or leaving by this main gate. One or two cars tried to rush us, but were turned back. Then we had half a dozen or so workers walking and pushing their way through. We felt that sitting or lying down was less provocative than standing, so we squashed together in three rows. Hilary was banged on the head by a bicycle being carried in, and a policeman trod on my stomach, not very hard I am glad to say! We tried to talk to the workers but they felt we were a load of unemployed layabouts so were not impressed. To be quite honest the workers were delayed as much by the press as they were by us, but at least no vehicles got in at all, and when we heard that helicopters had been used to transport vital people in, we felt we had had some success. We were also aware that if the police had really wanted to move us, there were more than enough of them to do so, which of course is exactly what happened at one gate at Greenham. In our four-hour stint we let in and out a few residents, but we were not entirely happy about this, as the houses are owned by the MoD and most people there work in the factory.

After about three hours of sitting on old fertiliser bags we began to get a bit chilly, but out observers kept supplying us with hot coffee, sandwiches, chocolate, etc., and we sang a few songs (rather badly) and sometimes sat back to back for a bit of support and a small area of warmth. Our main problems were the SWP crowd who paraded about with banners and newspapers purely for their own sakes. They had had no NVDA training, wanted to stand when the rest of us wanted to sit and were a damn menace. One CND member bought all their newspapers so we could sit on them, but the SWP girl rushed off to her van and came back with masses more. Then one of the NVDA instructors said that he would give them a briefing down the road, and when they returned, they were furious as they said it had been undemocratic and stupid, that much to our relief and cheers, they all pushed off.

By this time the sun was shining at intervals and no more people were attempting to go in or out. When the relief batch of CND members turned up for duty, we got to our feet and walked briskly back to camp, where we had breakfast. We were not on gate duty until 6pm, but on standby at 2pm. Luckily, we were not needed then, so some of our group went to Reading, Konrad played his guitar and the rest of us relaxed. There were masses of reporters at the site as Joan Ruddock, Bruce Kent, etc., were giving interviews. Konrad and I both gave recordings for the local radio, Konrad with his guitar and me with just talking. Unfortunately, we did not hear the end product, as we had no radio.

We had another meal and lots of wine at about 4.30 before going off to the Bluebell Gate. At about 5 the heavens opened and it bucketed down for about an hour. The campsite turned into a sea of mud, vehicles and people got stuck and the whole place was bedlam. We waited until the rain eased as everyone felt it was not a good idea to sit for four hours soaking wet on the road, although we felt bad about those getting wet at the end of a long stint. Bluebell Gate was not far away and we relieved a lot of drenched people. The police on duty here were very chatty as they stood in line looking down on us. I felt there was quite a lot of needle in their remarks, but Konrad and Richard who bore the brunt of it, did not rise at all. After about an hour different police came on and they were much more reserved. We were lucky not to get wet again, and although we sang a bit, the time passed slowly. It was a very small gate and when some demonstrators came early to relieve the sitters, we decided to go and put candles out along the road as by then it was very still and pitch black. On the walk back we met Mark who joined us, collected the candles and lit and stuck them in the banks. We had mulled wine & cake and went to our tents.

We all slept much better although there were one or two heavy squally showers. As there were many others campers by that time, we decided that we would do two hours blockading at Tulip Gate at the civilized time of 8am. This was much the most relaxed period: there was a wood fire for warmth, only a few police, no road for residents to drive down, and a crowd who could actually sing properly! There was a radio, so we heard what was happening in the world, and when we did the Hokey Cokey. One of the policemen very nearly joined us. Our two hours went rapidly and when we returned to the camp we rushed to take our tents down and get in the van and car to join the Chain, as we were informed that the road were filling up so fast, that if we didn't go soon we would have to stay at Burghfield.

We made a convoy of van, car and motorbike, and set off for the main road between Burghfield and Aldermaston. As we approached it, we met the traffic. Coaches, cars, pedestrians all jammed together. We had been feeling a bit isolated in our small group at the camp site, but when we joined this avalanche of people we were overwhelmed with a feeling of relief and exhilaration. It had been the same at Greenham in December. There is always a fearful period when you think you are the only people who have bothered to turn up. Well, we had this fantastic and very slow seven-mile drive to Aldermaston, with people both lining and filling the road. They all looked and pointed to the Peace Van, and cheered when we shouted that the road was solid with people behind us. Once we pulled up and asked a girl where she thought we should park. She didn't know where, but then rather shamefacedly she said that she had been the person who had recently got the Peace Van stuck in a multi-storey car park in Darlington! We went on until we were just past the Aldermaston main gate where we hoped that we might meet up with the Deal coaches. There were not quite so many people there, so we pulled off on to a side road and joined the crowd. By this time, it was just after one after one, but the organisers on bikes with megaphones said that there would be a delay in making the chain as many more demonstrators were still arriving. We lined ourselves up in a large puddle that helped to wash some of the Burghfield mud from our boots, and waited. We felt, as campers, we were easily distinguishable from the coach parties, by our weather-beaten appearance mad, mud, and scruffy slept-in clothing. After a while the megaphones boomed, bells rang, whistles whistled, and the balloons were let off. These balloons were not very great on our bit of road, as they either sank like stones, or else floated into the bare branches of the trees opposite, and just hung there. Local children had a marvellous time trying to rescue them later.

It was really a bit of a let down after this, no one knew quite what to do next. I suggested that as a gesture of defiance all the men should pee through the Aldermaston fence, but no one took the idea up. We walked back to the main gate, again searching for Deal people, and after hanging around for a while, decided that we would drive to the Festival site. At this point, Sue and Peter left us.

Luckily, Mark knew his way around the area, so we soon got off the crowded road. We did see Terry's empty coaches parked, but did not stop. We went round various lanes and then saw the Festival site from the back, across a large soggy meadow, so we parked and set off for it. Our only problem was a wide, water-filled ditch, but we negotiated quite well apart from Konrad with a hole in his boot. Again we searched for Deal's two banners unsuccessfully, so wandered round, let off special balloons for Liz and Eileen, met friends from other areas, watched and listened to the **Fall Out Marching Band**, street theatre groups, jugglers, children playing on the inflatables, singers, groups, speeches, etc., etc. We stayed for a couple of hours, went back to the van, had soup and set off for home. We dropped Mike in London, and I drove the rest of the way arriving in Deal at about 10pm.

Burghfield, Aldermaston, Greenham Common. For me, these names conjure up pictures of chain link fencing, barbed wire, strange igloo mounds, pipes and aerials, stark buildings and huts, neatly trimmed grass, MoD police and civil police, guard dogs, notices, military vehicles, oppression. We stood, sat, danced and sang to relieve our anxieties and fears that these places and all nuclear weapons produce. We want to show our solidarity, and for a few hours being with the thousands who feel as we do, were exhilarated, and gained strength from our mutual concern. We felt despair with one farmer in a 15 mile radius who would rent us a field for camping, but who charged CND £1,200 rental with a £2,000 deposit which would be forfeited if there was more than one campfire and too much wear and tear on the ground (in his opinion), which there must have been after that rain. Sitting on roads, forming human chains is all very well, but somehow I do not feel we are gaining many more supporters this way. Is it all just self-indulgence? The organisers worked hard, too hard somehow, spontaneity was lacking. Megaphones, instructions, roster sheets, etc. OK, you can't expect all those people to be in the right place at the right time by intuition only, and of course we were told that it was up to us where and when we blockaded, but all the same I felt we were being too organised. The SWP were a pain as they went purely for their own gain and profit. They certainly do not do the CND image any good.

Are we doing our cause and ourselves any good? I do not think we can go on making human chains round the countryside, or blockading unless on a massive scale with hundreds or thousands per gate. I feel that the December demo at Greenham was more successful, perhaps because it was the first, perhaps because it was all women. However, I am glad I went to Burghfield. The shared discomfort, cold, wet, etc., were necessary, and in our group, we looked after ourselves well. We were so prepared, that in some sort of way it was almost, but not quite, a disappointment not to be arrested.

But, where do we go from here?

29th October 1983

Down in darkest Deal we do not always hear what is happening in the rest of Britain; the grapevine network is slow to reach us. As far as I was concerned, the demo on 22nd October was OK and many people turned up in support, but by the time I had read the Sunday Observer and the Monday Guardian, I was in despair. I phoned Hilary on Monday early, and told her to read the paper before I came to see her in the afternoon. By this time, she was pretty gloomy too. In effect, we both felt that although somewhere between 200,000 and 400,000 people had turned up at Hyde Park, the powers-that-be and the media had more or less ignored us.

We decided to try a contact in Canterbury. How did they feel? It appeared there was a meeting that evening to discuss the cutting of the perimeter fence at Greenham Common on Saturday. Mind you, it was not put in those blunt terms, but we were invited to come along and find out what was happening. This direct action has been though up nearly a month earlier, but somehow no one had told us. The point was that only *'reliable'* women were contacted, and everyone hoped that the police and security would be increased on that day, although everyone was aware that the cruise build up would be starting at the base by 1st November. Telephone chats about what was going to happen were strictly forbidden, so there was a lot of foot slogging to arrange everything. At our meeting in Canterbury there were about 11 active women who were prepared to go, and they had already had their instructions and NVDA briefing. What we had to do was to drive to Greenham on the 29th Oct, and then we would be told how to proceed. As a cover we said we were going to a Halloween party! We took pumpkins as well as bolt cutters, but I do not think many people were deceived. Incidentally the code name for the cutters was *'black cardies'*, but I've no idea why. Hilary and I decided to join the Canterbury crowd and if possible get some women from Deal and Dover. I wanted to have a driver, as I did not feel capable of driving and cutting.

Our first problem was bolt cutters. We had been given a sample of perimeter fence, so we searched our own toolboxes. I found a fairly chunky pair of cutters, which we decided to test. Unfortunately, we mislaid our *'sample'* so in broad daylight wandered around trying to find a test fence. There are one or two odd cuts in a fence in Deal, which shall be nameless, but when we eventually found our sample, we realised that these cutters were useless. Well, from the sublime to the ridiculous we went. Through friends and many phone calls, we obtained on load the largest bolt croppers you have ever seen. They were a good four feet long, you had to have a licence to own them, and you needed a gorilla to lift them above shoulder height. (I also reckon they cost a bomb). Nevertheless, they cut the sample like butter red-hot. They were fantastic.

Problem number two was a driver. There were genuine reasons why Deal women whom we approached could not come, so in the end Pam and Janet from Dover joined us as driver and observers.

We all met at Canterbury, drove through London and met again ay the Heston Service station on the M4, to go in convoy to Greenham. Owing to roadworks (and as far as we could see, non-existent roadworks), we eventually reached Greenham at about 3pm, having seen quite a lot of women in cars and vans, all looking rather un-Halloweenish apart from a token pumpkin. As always at Greenham, it is so laid back and low key, it is never worth asking anyone what they want you to do, if you can even find anyone to ask. The only information I obtained was, that the cutting was to start at 4pm, and you just chose your own piece of fence and *got stuck in*. On our drive from the blue gate to the main, we were very daunted; I might be more honest and describe it as *shit scared*, by the number of police and British soldiers inside the fence. We were most terrified by the dogs they had, and that most of the men had walkie-talkies, so reinforcements could be called instantly to areas of action.

We parked our cars on the other side of the road opposite the main gate, met Vicky who lives at the camp now, but knows the Canterbury crowd. We decided that we would cut a couple of hundred yards from the main gate to the right, round the corner, so we went back to the car to get our cutters. The others just stuffed theirs under their jumpers and anoraks, but Hilary and I had a problem. I put our cutters down the leg of my jeans, and then put waterproof trousers over the top. I could only walk *very* slowly, with an extraordinarily bad limp, and they were damn heavy. They were so jammed down my jeans that when we got to the fence, in full view of the security people I had to strip-off to get them out!

Hilary and I cut like mad. We took it in turns, and I think it was only adrenalin that kept us holding those cutters above our heads. We cut on the diagonal all the time, as this makes the fence much harder to mend. I think we chopped about eight sections. An observer told me that they were photographing us from inside the fence while we were in action, and we were very aware that just a few yards from us there were half a dozen security police and an Alsatian dog. On each side of us cutting was going on, and about 50 yards away on the right, a whole section was pulled down and the police came out to grab the women. It was really quite hard to see what was going on as we were working so hard, cutting and pulling back cut pieces, taking it in turns all the time. The sweat was rolling off me and I hurled my jacket and sweater to Pam, and almost got down to my thermal vest! We did not really cut for all that long, 15 minutes or so, I have really no idea, it felt like hours, but we saw the security guards coming from where the fence was right down, so Hilary ran off with the cutters, as we knew they were the first things to be taken. As she rounded the corner she saw more police outside another wrecked section, taking bolt cutters from the women, and also arresting some. Hilary had the presence of mind to hide ours in the bracken under a silver birch, and when things were a little quieter, we found them again, tucked them under Hilary's jacket, wrapped my sweater round the bottom of them, and sneaked back through the bushes, over the road, and hid them in the car. We really felt we could not afford to have them taken by the police, and neither did we feel it was worth provoking arrest.

By this time I was shaking rather a lot, but I think it's better doing something so I held on to a section of fence which police and workmen were trying to repair from the inside, and we were trying to hold down from the outside. One of the coppers came out and grabbed me hard and heaved me down. I felt my fingers give out, so let go and landed with a bump. They got that section back up, but it was not very secure, and I think we all knew it would not take much to get it down again. One woman who obviously felt that arrest was the *right thing to do*, was inside the fence, lying down, with security guards taking no notice of her, at times walking right over her. By this time it was getting dark, so we went and had some nourishment and decided what to do next.

When we met up with the Canterbury women, we found that two of them had been arrested. One was acting as observer to a Cheltenham group who had no observer with them, so Anne was nicked with them. Hilary from Canterbury was actually caught in the act, so I suppose that was a fair cop, but we all felt that the arrests were done in a very random fashion indeed. You were just lucky if you were left alone. Sometimes the police came outside the fence, round the back, and arrested you, sometimes grabbed when there was a big enough hole to climb through and grab you from the front. We heard various stories about the different treatment received as well. Some police and soldiers were quite ok, fairly gentle and friendly. Others were very rough indeed, put the boot in, and I have heard since of at least one broken arm, bent-back wrists, etc.

Back at the main gate, we had quite a laugh. Before the cutting started, one woman poured Super Glue into the main padlock, and it worked a treat. The guards had to use a pair of bolt cutters, (with us outside giving advice on how to use them) to cut the padlock itself away, and replace it with a very small and inadequate one!

We decided we must cut again. Unfortunately, many of the cutters had been seized, but others had been hurled into the bushes. We found one pair, and by now in pitch dark, started again. Almost instantly torches were shone in our faces and the dogs started barking. A voice from inside the fence, coming from the direction of a torch being pointed at me, said, "I recognise that one", so I cut a moment longer and passed the cutters back to a waiting woman, and went back to the main gate to get more to come and help us. Quite a lot joined me and I led them back to our area. Slight panic when I got there as I found the Canterbury crowd, but not Hilary. Eventually she turned up and told us what had happened. She had waited quietly until it all went silent, and then started cutting on her own like mad. A dark shape appeared beside her, and grabbed her arm, so she hurled the cutters away. The policeman asked her where they were, and when she said she didn't know, much to her surprise he let go of her arm, and walked off, straight into a large area of brambles! She was really very lucky. A bit later, we went back to the spot with my torch, and she found her hat, but no sign of the cutters. The copper probably found them himself.

We all went back to our cars. The Canterbury women said that they would stay as long as necessary to find their two arrested friends, but they thought we could do no more good by staying so Pam, Janet, Hilary and I came home.

Neither Hilary, nor I, had wanted to leave. This sort of thing is a big problem. We felt we should stay on, but there were quite a lot of buts. First our cutters were so big, heavy and unwieldy, that we knew they would be seized if we used them again, and they must have been very expensive, so we wanted to return them. We thought all along that this was a one-day operation, and had told Pam and

Janet so, which meant they had commitments at home. We could not help the Canterbury women, apart from being supportive, as our car was full. In addition, there were many women going home at this time, and we thought the whole affair had come to a finish. However, I still felt we should have stayed on, and so did Hilary. OK next time we will.

I do not think the actual cutting was done correctly. We should have cut large triangles or diamonds in the fence. Large enough for someone to crawl through, and almost impossible to mend easily. Our cutters were super-efficient, but much too big. You want more cut and run tactics, with one person taking the cutters off you when threatened, and hiding them where they can be found again. The observers should really be far enough back to be out of the danger zone, but in the dark this is not possible. Having said this, I am not sure that cutters can ever be used again like this. New tactics are necessary, but do not worry: the Greenham women are thinking and working on it all the time.

31st October 1983

Another demo, this time in Trafalgar Square and Whitehall. The MPs were voting just down the road whether to have Cruise missiles in this country. Of course, it was a foregone conclusion, but thousands of us felt we must go to show our unhappiness, frustration, but not despair. We will go on protesting until the end.

Trafalgar Square was packed with people holding torches. A sight, once more to give us hope, that we are not alone. No one there knew what was planned as it is against the law to demonstrate near the Houses of Parliament when it is in session. I wandered off and found some women who had been at Greenham on Saturday, and they thought that we would all go in procession down Whitehall anyway. Quite by chance, our group found itself quite near the front of the procession, in with a large Christian group, punks and SWP. Just a few yards down Whitehall, there was a triple line of police with vans and reinforcements backing them up. We sat down in the road, and hundreds followed us, so the whole road back to the square was solid with sitting people. The Christians sang continuously, mainly protest songs, some religious, and after a couple of hours, not only was I hoarse, but almost converted! The singing was mainly to show our peaceful protest, and to drown out the more unruly element of SWP shouting inappropriate slogans. After a while, this group went off, I think to join some anarchists who were popping up behind the police cordon.

Bruce Kent, Jill Ruddick and other CND leaders were sitting near us and I think we all found the road hard after about 2 ½ hours. Apart from those sitting, the pavements were also packed, and I spotted Jill and Alan, whom Mark had met only a few days before at Hyde Park. We talked (or more truthfully shouted in each other's ears), exchanged news and agreed that we would probably meet again soon at another demo.

Soon after I saw women from Greenham appearing, hand in hand. They came right round between the sitting protesters and the police. I recognised Lee, an American whom I talked to earlier, and went and joined her in their line, standing with arms linked, and our backs to the police. I really felt that these were the people I *had* to be with. There is this curious kindred spirit, complete understanding and togetherness, mixed with the knowledge that over the weekend we had all broken the law and cut the fence. I don't know, it's hard to define, unless you experience it, perhaps it is a sort of mental rapport.   Anyway, a great cheer went up from the seated demonstrators. They passed candles to us and we stood, swayed and sang more songs, mainly Greenham ones, including "There's a hole in your fence, dear major...." At this, the whole crowd erupted, and even the police behind us laughed. Mind you, I am glad they didn't search us, as I'm certain most of us had a token piece of Greenham perimeter fence in a pocket or bag!

Soon after 10 Jill Ruddick asked everyone to go home quietly, and the seated ones got up and wandered back to Trafalgar Square, but the Greenham women formed themselves into a huge circle, still holding hands, having put the lighted candles on the road. We danced round in circles and snakes, sat down again in a ring, drew CND and feminist symbols on the road in chalk, and tried to organise a drifting off in twos and threes to meet again outside the Houses of Parliament. Actually the authorities had anticipated this and every street leading in that direction had anticipated this and every street leading in that direction was blocked by police, so I think we either drifted home (very reluctantly in most cases) or went straight back to Greenham whether prepared with sleeping bags etc., or not. I must say I was very tempted indeed to go with them. Each time I see them, the pull is stronger.

4th – 6th November 1983

This is not an easy weekend to describe to the folks back home. There was nothing dramatic happening at all. To be honest I would have to say we had a firework party, drank a lot of booze, went for some country walks, helped make two benders. We ate a lot of good food, drank rather scummy coffee, were interviewed by Finnish, Swiss, Yugoslavian & French journalists, had our photos taken many times (including at 8.30am) and got buzzed & surveyed by helicopters about every three quarters of an hour. We chatted and argued with police and soldiers, were a tourist attraction to hundreds of people who came to see us on Sunday, sang, danced and got a lot of smoke in our eyes from campfires. We crapped in the shit pit. I found my car quite comfortable to sleep in, and good to drive, but I had a major panic when a policeman went berserk and starting pulling tents and benders down. But, the real point of going to Greenham was communicating with the women. I think Hilary and I now feel that we are part-time residents of the Orange Gate.

We arrived at about 10pm on Friday night, found we had forgotten cooking utensils etc., but of course it didn't matter. We went straight to the campfire introduced ourselves, and sat and talked for about 3 hours. On our drive round the fence, we had seen hundreds more police and soldiers than last week, this time many outside as well as in. We realised that action was going to be difficult. The women said nothing had been planned for this weekend; it was a time to hear ideas, make friends with each other, relax, and try to make some sort of friendly contact with the security people.

The next morning we shared a huge breakfast of scrambled eggs with herbs, cheese etc., etc. and toast, then Hilary and I walked all along the fence to the main gate. It was really quite a sight. Almost every panel had been damaged in some way. We could see that many panels had been pulled right down; others had just been hacked about. Some had been mended in a fashion, but they would not take much unravelling to make women-sized holes to climb through. Inside now here are two rolls of barbed wire, but we thought these carefully snipped would pull back easily. The other little problem of course is the internal security. Every few yards, always in sight of each other are soldiers, and even in the remote spots, huge lamps and generators are set up. There is not a lot of privacy around the fence. This does not mean that the Greenham women have given up. *Just a change of tactics.*

At the main gate (Yellow), we handed over some money and talked for a while, but decided we far preferred the much more normal and less weird looking women at our gate. We went back, through the mud, over the duckboards, squeezing past policemen, most of whom really do look terribly young, had some lunch, and sat around. The clothes etc. that we handed over were very much appreciated the money also, and the *black cardie* raised a great laugh when I said, "it was donated by the Betteshanger miners". They had thought of having the handle inscribed, but reluctantly decided it would not be a good idea! On Sunday, Hilary and I had a discussion and agreed that it was no good keeping the cutters here in Deal, so we handed them over to Miranda for safekeeping, and she promised that she would make contact when they were going to be used, so we could help.

We decided to have a firework display that night, met the four from Canterbury, and two women from the Glastonbury Green Festival. There was rather too much sitting around with reporters etc., so when Miranda said she wanted to make a bender, we went and helped. The ground was very stony and hard and the only way I found to make holes was with a screwdriver and mallet. It worked. It took about an hour and a half to make the bender, a superior structure and we all felt very pleased with ourselves.

We then had supper, vodka and orange and lots of wine. A Swiss reporter had just been to Lamberhurst to do an article on English wine before coming to Greenham, so his presentation pack of three bottles were drunk almost before you had time to turn round. We then had the firework display. Well, not really a display, but we made the most of it with lots of "Ahhhhhhhs" etc., then we went up to the gate and sang and danced and argued with the security men, while about six women ran down the fence, just to see if that sort of diversion would make it possible for a break in. They thought it would. We were exhausted, went to bed and slept soundly. Mind you we were further away from the fence, but the benders are right alongside it, and they have to contend with the bright arc lights, loud remarks, changing shifts, etc. all night long from inside, with police driving vehicles and walking around, outside.

The next morning Liz brought us coffee in bed. How about that for luxury living! We decided not to bother with breakfast but have brunch instead. Hilary and I went for a walk on the common. It is lovely, very wild but sometimes nature is red in tooth and claw. We saw a rabbit being chased and caught by a stoat, only a few feet from us, and the screams of the rabbit were terrible. We tried to chase the stoat away, but it is impossible to know what happened in the end. The bad part of the common was suddenly coming on a great battery of lights to guide planes to the end of the runway. This really was an intrusion of privacy on English common land.

Another huge meal based on Bill's eggs, onion, tuna, and toast, which by this time I had learned how not to burn, and then once more reporters and hundreds of people turned up including a coach load from Wales. Some brought fuel, some food, some just words of encouragement, and some just walked around photographing us. Most were made to feel very welcome and their support was encouraging, but unfortunately there was an incident with some men who wanted to make a camp at the Orange Gate and join in any action that was going. All the women from the camp said that Greenham is *women only* and must remain that way and I agreed with them.

The Canterbury women were packing up their tent and getting ready to go and Hilary and I felt that we would probably leave shortly, but life at Greenham is never predictable. Things always happen. One nice thing that happened was that an Australian woman, Zohl, brought around a marvellous Pine Gap ring, decorated with mementoes from Greenham, which she was taking out to Australia, to a camp that was being set up near the uranium mines in the centre of the country. For about 2 years I have had a very worn down shell in my pocket which I picked up at Sandwich Bay, so this was hung on with gold thread, weaved in with the other wool and objects in a web shape, and the ring was held in a circle with some Greenham perimeter fence. I really like the thought of that all going to Australia. The next nice thing was that Diana asked Hilary and me to help her make another bender. Of course, we accepted the invitation gladly and went off with her and Miranda to get wood. Hilary and I took some back, and started to make the eight holes when two coppers picked up our branches and chucked them into the gorse. Oh God, we felt fools watching them do it, but when the others came back with more we retrieved most of it and set to work again.

Just as we finished, and stood back admiring our work another policeman came along and starting very roughly pulling down the tent next to the bender, and said he was going to take down all the dwellings next to the fence. Panic stations! Some of us rushed to our cars and raced to the main gate to collect women in support to argue with the police. They came running, but luckily, by the time we got back everything was normal. It appears that the policeman did this entirely on his own without any orders. His inspector was very annoyed with him and told him that by law, he was actually correct in what he did, but the police let a certain amount of latitude prevail as long as certain rules were obeyed by the women, one being that there must be a space between the benders and the fence.

By this time it was getting really quite late, so Hilary and I put the rest of our stuff in the car, collected up two women who wanted a lift to London, and drove home.

So, that was our weekend at Greenham Common. No fence cutting, only one woman inside and that was near the main gate, where they wanted to see if it could be done, nothing dramatic, but by being there entirely satisfactory and fulfilling. We have been told that any time we come again to the Orange Gate there will be room for us in a bender and we will always be made welcome. It is of course, an extraordinary life style, but once you have stayed there and become part of it, I can understand how this becomes the real world, not how everyone else lives. I shall go back on the 24th November to support Canterbury Hilary in her court case, if not before. We really do feel we shall overcome by our strength and togetherness.

23rd – 26th November 1983

I wasn't going to go to Greenham until very early on the Thursday morning, but the weather was so cold, and there was a chance of freezing fog, so I left on Wednesday afternoon, having done shopping, cooked a vegetable risotto, found clothes, two sleeping bags, hot water bottle, etc., etc. It was a long and not very pleasant drive on my own, but about three hours later when I arrived it was all worth it. The Greenham aura/magic/feeling was all there. Anyway, it is always nice to go back somewhere where you are known and wanted. I was greeted by Miranda, Ruth, Carola, Juliette, Rebekha, Charlie, Sian, Sally, Jane, Margaret, two Dutch women, a German called Elsa, a Dubliner, etc., etc. I produced the Orange Gate bowl I had made and they were all thrilled and passed it from hand to hand. Then I brought out Ruth's cake from Mongeham, and a bottle of wine, and we were away. Another cake was found and we had that, then more drink appeared, and I brought out the risotto. We just heated that up, and passed the saucepan round, and each dug in with our own spoons. It is a very formal life style there! Then Miranda insisted that she made up my bed in a free bender, as she was afraid I would be cold (there was a thick and very foggy frost). It was Diane's bender, which Hilary and I had helped to make 3 weeks ago, and I must say it is a splendid construction. Eventually we drifted off to bed, and after about half an hour, two other women arrived and slept in the same bender with me. At one point in the night, one of them screamed in agony with cramp in her leg, but overall it was quite peaceful, apart from the police tramping back and forth, vehicles passing, and the fact I was so hot I had to throw off clothes and blankets all night. I will not say I slept soundly, but I was fine and comfortable.

The next morning I crawled out of the bender, leaving the other two sleeping soundly. Actually, I never met them at all, as by the time I got back from the court they had left orange gate. At the campfire, there were a few people around and I had orange juice and coffee. At that moment, Hilary and Liz from Canterbury arrived, so we all went in convoy to the Newbury Magistrates Court. I took Jane, who had to appear, plus Sian and one Dutch woman, the other one going with Liz and Hilary. At the court, the busiest place was the 'Ladies'. It was entirely taken over by Greenham women who took advantage of the hot water in the basins to strip down, have a proper wash, and some even had the forethought to bring shampoo for their hair. It was really quite a sight. I had washed and cleaned my teeth earlier at the camp in ice crystals rather than water, so I realised these were the experienced Greenham women. Then we all stood and sat around outside court No.2 on the landing for hours. There were babies and women everywhere. The police and officials had to step over and round us to carry on their normal work, while we sat on the floor and drank WVS coffee at 10p per cup. The women who had to go before the magistrates were understandably rather apprehensive as they were charged with criminal intent and criminal damage. In the end, they all were referred to the Crown Court to appear on the 30th January. There were about 35 being charged and eventually they and their supporters all went back to the various gates at Greenham. Hilary, Liz and I sat talking and rather wondering what to do next, when suddenly two or three cars drew up near the campfire and a hoard of American and English women got out, and starting taking food from their cars. It was Thanksgiving Day and they had brought a banquet for the Greenham women! You have never seen such food in your life. Quiches, four or five different salads, corn bread, muffins, olives, pumpkin and apple pies, the lot. Plus, masses of red and white wine. We could not believe our eyes. They had brought plates, glasses, knives and forks, everything. Well, for most of the rest of the day, we sat, ate, drank and talked. Other people turned up as well, including a woman with an accordion who played and sang to us. Eventually Liz and Hilary felt they had to go back home, so I saw them off and then came back to the party.

I must try to explain. This is all part of the Greenham 'thing'. A great deal of strength is gained on both sides by the arrival of perhaps one woman, or a coachload. While we had been at the court, a woman from London had turned up, and had done all the washing up (which was a hell of a lot I must admit) then gone again. Another woman in a Rolls Royce drove up with some food, sat and talked to us and had a coffee, then departed. Another woman in a fair sized car, parked it, opened the boot, which was full of firewood, which she proceeded to dump on our woodpile, had a coffee and a talk and drove off. It happens all the time, I had only been in Greenham for weekends before and thought this communication only happened then, but it doesn't, it happens all the time. On Friday, a national coach, driven by a woman, came from Wales for the day. They all had parcels of food or goods, asked us if they could photograph us for a primary school project which one of the teachers was doing, and tins of fruit or jars of coffee had children's labels on, saying "With love to Greenham women from Caroline, Joan and Anne, aged 7". Two men arrived and were very diffident about approaching us, but were delighted when we asked to them to have a coffee and sit with us for a while. Oh yes, another family came with chairs to put round the campfire. The feeling of helpfulness and kindred spirits and air of peacefulness and community of experience is something I have never come across in this way before. I think many of the ordinary police feel this. One drove up in his car when we were making a kitchen bender, and said it was a fantastic construction and "could he please take a photo of it?" Another policeman asked me whether we had had a bad night with the gale and he hoped we were all right. He said that he was glad that the squaddies had gone as he thought that they were not the right people to guard the base against women. He said he knew that we would go inside again, and was obviously extremely sympathetic. He could not say too much, but I think communication with the sort of copper who is prepared to listen and not just think we are all lunatic women is very important. Letters arrived on Friday, some addressed specifically to the orange gate. Twenty pounds was in one envelope, words of support in others, and prayers for peace from all over the place. The people who come in person all want to feel that they are part of Greenham Common, and they are, whether they stay for an hour or a year. The women who live there all the time do get quite exhausted at the constant flow of visitors and find it hard to get any time to themselves, and even the short times I have been there I am exhilarated but also drained. I need a re-charge quite often though.

Eventually I crawled into the bender. This time Carola shared it with me. It was a much milder night and I hurled off even more blankets. It is lovely to lie in a bender and look up at the branches still with leaves on them. It is quite light in them as the arc lights shone all night. I was wakened sometime during that night by a great roar outside, but Carola informed me that it was "just one of the unfriendly cops", who resented the fact that the women were asleep, so every now and then made a loud noise to wake us all up. On well, you can't win them all.

I got up about 9am and had some breakfast. There were a fair number of thick heads around, and some women did not appear until about midday. Miranda and I decided to go to Thatham to do some shopping, mainly for fresh milk and newspapers. It is only when you stand in a crowded Co-op that you are aware of the odd aroma coming from yourself and your Greenham companion. Mostly wood smoke I think, but I can understand how the locals notice us. We notice their over-strong smell of perfume, and somehow they really do look different from Greenham residents. Miranda was not a bit well, she had flu and back at the camp kept disappearing off to her bender with foul concoctions of crushed garlic and hot orange juice, (I never noticed the smell funnily enough) and I dozed in the car for an hour.

When I came to, it was starting to drizzle, so Ruth, Carola and I decided it was time we made a high bender to go over the campfire and seats, as being continually soggy is no fun. We rather ignored the usual visitors, apart from asking them to hold the odd thing, and got on with it. More digging of holes in that awful ground for me with the screwdriver, but eventually we were successful and had a proper shelter to sit under. It was great. Someone else made some supper and I produced my last bottle. We talked about *black cardies*, Christmas decorations and had a pleasant evening, but all the time the wind was picking up. By the time I went to the bender it was blowing a hurricane. For most of the night I ignored the noise quite successfully. In the morning, Miranda said she heard me snoring during the night! Carola and I both went in and out of the bender without waking the other. She told me that she didn't get to bed until about three as she had been trying to hold down the kitchen tent in the gale. I had to get up at some time to have a pee, Carola got up to get a drink of water, but the bender was covered with a tent fly sheet and this was banging so much, that any other noise was positively quiet, and we certainly never noticed crawling over each other's feet. At about 8.30 I got up properly and Carola did mutter something about "chaos in the kitchen area" as the tent had completely blown down.

The rain had stopped by this time thank goodness, and Ruth was up making coffee. Oh God, *what a mess*. The bender we had put up a few hours earlier, they had had to take down, all the cushions were sopping wet, as were wooden seats, chairs, food, everything. Ruth and I decided to make a start after breakfast, hoping that more would turn up by that time to help us. It all took a long time, sorting out good from bad. Actually very little of it was really bad, even the biscuits were OK at one end of the packets, and when I tried to chuck out some really grotty bits of butter and marge, I was promptly told that if the ashes and mud were scraped off, they would be fine. We decided to store some of the food in the *'pantry'*, a construction next to the benders, of bins and things under polythene. The only trouble was that the sheeting had blown back so the bins of fruit, vegetables, more biscuits, etc., had an inch of water in the bottom of each container. Well eventually we got it all straightened out to some degree or order, and then Carola who was getting a lift back with me as far as London, asked if I was in a hurry, as if not she thought we ought to make a kitchen bender, rather than just put the tent up again. We used all the material from the camp fire bender, I dug six more holes with the screwdriver, then we made a trench all round for the surplus polythene to be tucked in with earth piled on top, made fastenings with stones tied inside a bunched piece of sheeting, with a brick hung like a parcel from the outside. We had diagonals as well as struts, and it really was a masterpiece. I hope it still is, because that night the next gale came and I am terrified that if the wind got inside it, it could never get out and the whole thing would have taken off like a giant balloon. Ruth is the most practical one there; let us hope that she will have looked after it!

One strange thing happened while we were having lunch. Six men in ordinary clothes and one policewoman in uniform came out of the base and over to us, and asked if we would give them a cup of tea. We asked them what they did in the base, and they were very cagey indeed, and would not say, just asked us questions. We did not like them at all, so quite soon they moved off. They were obviously special branch, particularly as they kept asking about the German woman who had gone by that time. Most visitors are welcome, but not quite all, especially if they come out of the base.

Carola and I left at about 2.30, and I got home about 3 hours later. I cannot wait to go back there on the 9th December.

9th – 13th December 1983

Hilary and I had a long, dark, wet and windy drive to Greenham on Friday evening, not getting to the Orange Gate until 11.30. There was only one woman still wandering around, so we had a drink and went to bed in the car. It was still blowing like mad and we felt it would be noisy in a bender and anyway it's hard to knock on bender '*doors*' and ask if there is any room inside, although I did try.

The next morning we met old friends and new ones, and all day women were arriving. There were 270 Americans from Minnesota over for 9 days to meet Greenham women in the demonstration and give general support. They had been sponsored by women's groups from back home, who paid the airfares. They came, I think, because they were so ashamed of Reagan. They also support their own Peace Camps in USA. One of the permanent residents at the Orange Gate is Sally and on Saturday morning, a car drew up with Americans in it asking for her. Her mother had arrived before her letter to say that she was coming. We found Sally. She and her mother Barbara had a fantastic time talking, and Barbara moved into Sally's bender, and was still there when I left.

Preparations were being made all round us for the following day's demo. There were plenty of troops inside the fence, and far more police that I had seen last time I was there. On outside, marquee tents and loose were being erected. Hilary and I were quite surprised that the demo was not just going to be with mirrors, musical instruments, etc., but we were going to try to get the fence down again. There was quite a lot of discussion where this should take place, and of course, we said that we would do what we could to help. I was not sure what the reaction of some of Deal people would be to this, but they did not have to join in. They were coming up in a mini bus and the Peace Van just for the day on Sunday, and there were children with them, including Esther.

In the afternoon, Hilary and I drove round to the Green Gate, which neither of us had seen before. It is very lovely, quiet, and peaceful in the woods, with lots of tents there, but the silos are very close, which makes the reality inside the fence very real and overpowering. There was meant to be a mixed demo at that gate on the afternoon we were there, but apart from the fact there were quite a lot of men with the women wandering round the fence, nothing much seemed to happen and there was a strong Christian element around. The Buddhist nuns were chanting and when a couple of them recognised us, they carried on beating their instruments and just bowed to us. We bowed back, what else does one to under such circumstances?

We went back to the Orange Gate, where we were given instructions as to how to use the *'baby'*. This is a ratchet-and-lever thing that is hooked to the fence on one side, and round a sturdy tree on the other with a length of rope. The idea is to pull down the fence down (hopefully). There were obviously going to be problems with it, so that night when it was dark, about 6 of us went on to the Common where the runway feed-in lights are, and tried it out on two of the posts. We certainly got them to bend, but I think we felt it was going to be a slow operation, but with the cutting with *'knitting needles'*, the *'tea party'* could probably take place. Also, we hoped that there would be so many women around that our activities would not be spotted too soon.

We had some supper and a bit of a party, a sing-song and a dance with Marion playing her accordion and giving barn dance instructions, which on frozen ground and in a rather alcoholic haze were not all that easy to follow. Eventually we went off to the car to sleep, and were glad of all the sleeping bags and blankets we had, as it was freezing hard by this time, and trips to the shit pit were decidedly chilly. I had left some orange juice in the car door pocket. In the morning, this was frozen hard, as were all the windows on the car on the inside. Cleaning teeth in the morning in ice crystals that will not pour out of the container takes some doing, but personally I would much rather have cold still air rather than wind, which cuts right through you.

We had breakfast, and all morning women arrived, most of them bearing gifts of some sort, clothes, blankets, food, drink, money: £300 to the orange gate alone. There were piles of plastic bags everywhere. The place looked a hell of a mess, but we just piled it all into the washing tent and the kitchen bender and left it there for the time being. Much to our surprise, the police were letting vehicles come to all the gates, so we kept an eye out for the Peace Van, and Hilary and I walked down to the road to see if it had arrived. First, I saw Melanie and Robert who had brought a vine to plant, then I met Jill Tweedie, Alan Briers, Jane and a friend, and I took them back to the camp and introduced Hill to various residents. Diana showed her the bender that I had helped to make. Then I saw Sian and Cleise wandering off round the fence and I joined them as we decided to find a good place to use the *'baby'*. We were told that some London women had brought 100 *'knitting needles'* with them so we dispersed some of these round the place, and then walked towards the Main Gate, and decided that the area around the swamp was the best area for fence pulling and cutting, as it would be hard to get police reinforcements there. Mind you, by this time, more and more police were moving into position, but also more and more women were stationing themselves round the fence and we were obviously going to have a fantastic turnout. We knew some of these were prepared to be active, but we had no idea how many.

We went back to the Orange Gate, having fixed our spot, and there I met Elizabeth and Kirstie with the children. By this time it was 1 o'clock and suddenly the whole place erupted with noise. Shouting, banging, musical instruments being played, (I hooted the car horn, and others copied me) and for about 5 minutes, there was this amazing noise everywhere. The papers estimated about 30,000 women, but as usual, it is impossible to tell. All I know is that there were one-hell-of-a-lot around where I was.

By 2 those prepared for action, Sian, Zoe, Cleise, Charlie, Rebekah, Annie, Margaret, Sally, Ruth, Hilary, Penny, Jean, Miranda, Diana, Nikki, Gerry, Marion, Shirley, Leslie, me, etc., etc., etc. collected our knitting needles, and went off down the fence. We decided our action should take place at 3 o'clock. We found a really muddy, mucky spot, and stood around and some sat down where the *'baby'* was going to be fixed on to a tree, and just as the yelling and shouting started, we made for the fence. I cut like hell, and just as a policeman was about to grab the cutters, I chucked them behind me to someone else. An Inspector was going up and down the line of women with his men trying to stop us, but we went on cutting, but then got the idea of pulling the fence, just by womanpower. My God, *it worked!* I think we all thought that those posts were sunk 10 feet into the ground. They are not! The fence shook and wobbled, and swayed. The baby was captured and hurled inside, but it didn't matter. We just heaved in unison, and while we heaved, the cops pulled us off, but we went back, again and again. A burly policeman sat on top of me, but I still had my fingers inside the fence, pulling all the time. Then a section with post came down, and I saw Sian, Charlie and others chuck some carpet over the barbed and razor wire, and climb in for their *'tea party'* and stand on top of the hill waving their arms. Some soldiers grabbed them, but instead of making arrests, shoved them back outside to us, over the wire again. The police were getting rough, so we moved a few yards away, and went on pulling and more fence gave. At one point, I was being pulled by a policeman from outside and a soldier was thumping my knuckles from the inside, but I hardly felt it. Most times when I was hurled off, the women standing and encouraging us caught me, but once I went with a crash on my back. By this time, we were all covered with mud, which was almost knee high in places anyway. The police linked arms and tried to lean against the fence to stop it coming down, so for a few minutes, I put my arms each side of a helmet and unravelled the wire round his head. When I was exhausted and realised I could not do much more, I went and found Hilary and we squelched our way back to the Orange Gate. Diana came with us, and although large sections of the fence had not been touched, back at the Orange Gate we met up with more of the Deal party and when I saw the fence swaying there, Diana and I went up to it and started all over again until once more we were worn out. I felt as though my arms had been pulled out and the knuckles on my right hand were swelling fast. By this time, it was quite dark apart from the arc lights, and most of the activity was dying down.

I did not want to go. This always happens to me. To hell with the cold, muck, discomfort etc., etc. it's people who count, and once I get to Greenham, I forget everything and just want to stay on. The people back in the real world say it's like a drug, I suppose they're right. Anyway, I found Hilary and the others, and they said I should stay. But Hilary had to get back so she joined the others in the Peace Van, 14 by this time, as some had walked from the main gate. So, she took her things and went off with them. I was sorry to see her go, but she has commitments and now I have shed mine. It's taken a hell of a long time, but I think at last I've done it.

I did not want to sleep in the car on my own, so Zoe said I could share her bender and Anne Marie was there as well. Luckily, I had the sense to put my things in 'Bender 13' quite early on in the evening, as I can't remember what happened later on. I do remember we had supper, and a lot to drink, and Miranda took me for a walk on the Common in the freezing cold to try and straighten me out, but I can't remember what she said or why. The next thing I can clearly remember is being shoved more to one side in the bender as I was taking up too much room, and that I had a hot water bottle in my sleeping bags. It appears that Rebekha had put me to bed, then worried that I might be cold, so made a hot water bottle in my sleeping bag. I do have vague sort of memories about this, but nothing is at all clear. Mind you, I do not think I was the only woman in this state. My only (weak) excuse is that it was a reaction to the day's activities.

During the night I was aware of a sprinkling noise on the bender, and when Anne Marie decided to get up, she pulled aside the polythene door and there was the world white with snow. It looked beautiful, but cold. Zoe and I stayed in bed and Anne Marie brought us coffee, so we sat and smoked and talked for an hour or so. She told me a bit about her life as a single parent, and her problems of bringing up her daughter on her own. Her daughter is now 14 ½ and had been there the day before but had gone back home and to school. It has not been an easy life for Zoe, but she, like me, gains enormous strength from Greenham.

The back of my neck was quite painful, and for a little while I did wonder if I was suffering my first hangover, but as some days later is still hurts, I think it is more likely that the pulling and being hurled to the ground, was the cause. Eventually we got up and went to the campfire. God, *the place a mess*! The gifts, given us the day before, were everywhere with a sprinkling of snow and ice on the ones outside the shelter and with mayhem, dirty dishes and pans everywhere. After breakfast we started cleaning up. It took us most of the day, but we took it in turns. I saw a pair of red waterproof trousers which I put on, as John's which I had worn the day before were completely covered in gritty mud. I felt really smart with these on. Sian asked me if I would take her and Nikki to Newbury station as Nikki was not well, and a Dutch woman wanted to go to the Red Gate to find some friends. At Newbury train station it as nice to use a proper loo and wash some of the filth from my hands in hot water, but obviously a lot of Greenham women had been there, as a roller towel was really grotty, and the loo paper had run out. I said goodbye to Sian (who was going to Bath for a bath). I did some shopping in Newbury, and was rather conscious of my appearance, but in the Peter Dominics Off-Licence, I felt more at home, as it was full of Greenham women, looking and smelling like me. I picked up the Dutch woman, and went back to the Orange Gate, where I saw Diana and told her there were: "No Guardians left in Newbury".

We had some lunch. A woman rushed over and said she had just seen Diana being chased through the woods by a police officer as she had been cutting the fence with Zuphie. Well there was nothing we could do for the time being, so we carried on tidying-up and talking. Then Penny came back in a state. She had gone up the road to make a phone call, when a man had stepped out of the bushes on the Common and exposed himself. We went in a bunch to confront him. Of course, we did not find him, but we waited outside the phone box for ages with an American woman who was making calls to the States for hours. On our way back, we realised that there was a lot of stuff left by the demonstrators and stalls etc., so I went back for the car, and piled loads of sopping wet polythene, and a water container, and took it back to the camp. I don't think the car will ever recover, but why worry! A lot of the women had left by this time, and there were only about 15 or 16 of us left. For the first time, I got very cold that evening, and I had to make rather frequent trips to the shit pit, which did not help much, and my neck was hurting like hell. None of us felt much like drinking, but we found a bottle of Bristol Cream and some dates, so we had that our aperitif, and it went down well. The wind was picking up, so we wrapped ourselves in blankets and got tucked in for a quiet social evening. The one problem was what had happened to Diana and Zuphie? A couple of the women went down to the phone, and the cops denied all knowledge of them. We were going to go round all the gates and see if they had turned up there, but Miranda said leave it for an hour or so, as she was certain they'd turn up. Five minutes later they arrived! They had been arrested and eventually let out, had fish and chips and took a taxi back to Orange Gate, but the story of their adventures is too long to put here.

We were all tired, and went off to bed with a hot water bottle quite early. I had the bender to myself, but Zoe was coming back on Wednesday to go to court, so I promised I would look after it for her.

I did not sleep at all well. At about a quarter to two I had to get up, put on boots and jacket, and got for a shit, and my neck was really painful. I looked for some painkillers in the car, and was very conscious of being watched by the security people, and as the back lock would not work, I pretended it did. I could not find any painkillers but went back to the bender and did sleep quite well, until the usual early morning insults and stones were hurled. A stone crashed against the bender, which was frightening but no worse than the shouts of "Get up you fucking, gobbing, smellies..." etc., etc. I felt very vulnerable in a bender on my own, but I knew that I had support round me and when the usual chopper flew low round and round us, it was time to get up. I was going home on that day, so I tidied up the bender and left Zoe a *'thank you for having me'* note attached to her hat.

I had some nice settling porridge for breakfast with coffee, and arranged with Cleise and Lesley that we would leave soon after 11 o'clock as we all had things to get back to. Diana said that they would make a bender for Cleise at Christmas and one for me when I came back for the New Year. It was said saying goodbye especially to the Americans who had to go back home, but even they said they would be here again before long.

One thing that amused us all on Tuesday morning was that the American servicemen were very busy trying to repair the damage done on Sunday. Groups of men went round with trucks, pieces of wire, and particularly interesting, large baulks of timber to shore up the leaning posts and torn fences. We wandered over to look at the work, and when I saw the timber, I said in a loud voice that we would no longer have trouble in getting firewood for the campfire at the Orange Gate. They were not amused.

I should mention that a lot of us had felt it had been an odd night. Penny had had some extraordinary dream about bending metal and being blood sisters, and holding a bridge, and I was very puzzled when I went to the car in the morning to find my piece of Greenham fence which is tied to the mirror, lying on the floor of the car, with the ribbon actually untied. Explain that one away!

We got away at about 11.30 and for a long time were quite silent in the car. I think it affects me in this way, but then Cleise talked about her life, and told me about her working class background, how she been in the women's army nursing corps, etc., and how she had felt an outsider as an unmarried woman in most places apart from Greenham. I dropped her off at Earls Court, and took Lesley back to Canterbury. I know we will meet again soon.

12th December 1983: Diana's Story

On Monday, when the clearing up and sobering up was taking place at the Orange Gate, Diana and Zuphie went for a walk to stretch their legs and look at the leaning, battered fence. Quite by chance, they happened to have a pair of cutters each on them, although they really had no intention of doing anything except look. Unbelievably there was a piece of comparatively undamaged fence, and not a cop in sight. The temptation was too great. Out came the cutters, and in no time at all a large hole appeared... then a police car. Diana did not see the police and strolled away into the woods (or so she said). The story we heard back at the gate was that Diana was last seen running like hell with a large policeman in hot pursuit! Anyway, Diana and Zuphie got caught, had their bolt cutters taken from them, and were driven to the Newbury cop shop. The ride was not pleasant as the security guards kept throwing open the windows of the vehicle, holding their noses and complaining loudly and rudely about the *'smellies'* and how the whole place stank because of them. This did not please Diana at all, but she was even more horrified when Zuphie muttered that they would have to turn out their pockets at the reception desk. Now Diana is a very well bred and brought up young woman and keeps certain functions as private as possible. So that morning, when she had to change her tampon, she did it in the privacy of her bender, and wrapped the used one in a great wad of tissues, and left it in her pocket to dispose of in the shit pit at her leisure. Unfortunately, she had either forgotten all about it, or had not found the time to do this, so she realised that unless she could execute a swift sleight of hand, all those unpleasant remarks about *'filthy women'* and *'smellies'* would be seen as true.

In the police station, she and Zuphie were told to turn out their pockets. At Greenham Common, women do not walk about with handbags, and therefore pockets are inclined to become rather cluttered. Diana borrowed Zuphie's gloves (she only had mittens-with-no-fingers herself) put them on, shoved the offending object inside, removed the gloves from her hands, and left gloves and hidden tampon shoved up one finger, on the desk. It took quite a long time to empty her pockets and each item had to be entered by the officer. Quantities of tissues, string, a penknife, two teabags (unused), bits of paper, a pencil, two tampons (unused), money, etc., etc. By this time, she was getting quite bold and actually asked to have the two clean tampons back, but there was still the problem of the one in the glove. She picked up the gloves, fiddled a bit with them for a moment, extracted the tampon, hid it in her now empty pocket without being seen, and put the gloves back on the counter. The officer was suspicious, picked up the gloves and tried to get his large hands in them, and when he found he could not, asked a WPC to check them. She made some funny sort of remark about "was he frightened a mouse would jump out?", but of course found nothing in them. The officer then asked Diana to read the list carefully detailing her belongings, but she told him he had forgotten detailing her belongings, but she told him he had forgotten to include the two tampons. Very seriously, he added them, and then she signed the list. Signing anything took rather longer than usual as Diana had given her full name as Diana *Greenham* Smith, and it takes a bit of thought to remember to add that Greenham in the middle.

To add to these complications Zuphie was going through the same procedure but had not given her proper name, as she wanted to go home to Europe for Christmas and return to England later. She had already been arrested before, so this time called herself something like Shirley Primrose and Diana kept forgetting and addressing her as Zuphie, then changing it to Shirley. It must have caused a lot of confusion, but even more so was the fact that the policy of Greenham women is, when arrested give no information except name and address. Diana found she could not do this and informed us it was nervousness that made her talk all the time. She told the police about her family, her divorce, the fact that her mother and sister had both been arrested, and should she admit to previous offences against the MoD fence at Greenham etc., etc. The police for pretty bored with all this, and when she was actually being charged, she was warned that there was not much space on the charge sheet, so she would have to keep her reason for damaging the fence very short. Diana thought for a moment and then at dictation speed said: "I cut a large hole in the fence to make easy access for others". This was not a popular statement to make.

The worst part of the afternoon was when Diana and Zuphie were shut away in separate cells. Diana felt very low with the four walls blankly looking at her, but when she examined them rather more closely, she found that other Greenham women had been there and scratched messages and names all round. These had to a certain extent been scrubbed out, but many were made and cut with a sharp implement, and were just legible. The only tool Diana had which would make any impression was the metal end of her bootlace, so she undid it, and scratched 'Di was here', and felt much more cheerful.

The interview with the inspector was a fiasco. Diana was still very chatty and did not behave in the way that he expected or wanted. To make matter worse, his wife phoned and Diana enjoyed the one sided conversation, particularly as she was obviously listening with much interest, so he turned his chair round half way, talked as softly as possible, and screwed his body and legs as far from her as possible.

As the conversation went on, embarrassment oozed from every pore:

> *"I'm sorry I'll be a bit late tonight."*
> [.............................]
> *"Yes, you're right."* (This was obviously in answer to a question about Greenham women making him work long hours.)
> [.............................]
> *"What's for supper?"* Cheerful voice
> [.............................]
> *"Cheesy mince? But I don't like that, if it's the same as last time. I told you I didn't like it then."* Gloomy voice.
> [.............................]
> *"Well, as long as it's not the same, I expect I'll like it."* Very doubtful voice.
>> At this point Diana was tempted to leap to her feet, grab the phone from his hand and tell the wife she should not put up with such criticism and treatment from a man. *Come and join the women and get liberated!* It's a good thing she resisted the temptation, as I can't think what the charge for inciting wives from inspector husbands would be, but I think the sentence would be very long.
> [.............................]
> *"Well I won't be all that long. Don't forget to unhitch the horse."*

End of conversation. He turned and faced Diana again.

The bit about unhitching the horse was a real puzzle. Apart from being a coded message at which the mind could boggle, (was the wife meant to dress up in drag as the back half of a horse?) Was it to ask her to open the garage door? Did he really have a horse that needed unhitching? (In the pitch dark?) Any clues as to the real meaning would be most welcome.

Eventually Diana and Zuphie were released after a date had been fixed for their court case. I should mention one other rather ludicrous happening. Diana had made a complaint during her hours of captivity about the behaviour of the security guards who had arrested them. She did not do it in the normal way. She stated she was furious and nobody should have to put up with that sort of verbal abuse. She would write to the newspapers and tell them about it. In fact, she had met Jill Tweedie only the day before and would contact her about it. At this point Zuphie who was only half listening to the tirade, piped up and stated that she had actually slept with Jill Tweedie the night before, then said "Oh no, wrong Jill".

I do not think the police at Newbury enjoyed their afternoon with Diana and Zuphie, and sometimes I *can* understand why Greenham Women are not popular with everyone.

29th Dec 83 – 1st January 1984

My arrival coincided with a meeting round the campfire, discussing a press statement to be put out the next day. The basic problem was that at the Orange Gate £1,000 had been received in donations over the Christmas period, and what should be done with the money? There were about 20 women in the group and after quite a long time - when each woman had a chance to have her say without interruption – the consensus was that a percentage of the money should go to women's groups worldwide. A few felt that court costs, publicity, postage and general living would eat into the cash received very quickly without giving any away. Some thought that Christmas was the only time when money was received in any quantity and reminded the group that last summer they were so short of money at Greenham that the office could not afford to send out letters asking for help for more. These points were well thrashed out, and apart from anything else, now that the telephone tree was in operation, if Greenham women for desperate for cash, a call to supportive women would surely raise more. The details of the statement were worked out, Sian said that she would very much like to administer it, and we agreed that it must not be seen or thought of as charity, but sharing. The oppressed groups could be in this country or anywhere else in the world, but big organisations such as Oxfam would not be considered as too much money was wasted in admin costs. 50% of money given to us was also agreed on, and the next morning the statement was written up, once again as a group effort, and was taken to the press conference. It is quite interesting to note that not all the women from other gates agreed with what we had done, as they felt it made the different gates too autonomous, but accepted that we had the right to do this if we felt like it. The other gates had a much more general statement about the struggle at Greenham with the Government and police which is getting stronger and more violent rather than less after 2 ½ years of peace campaigning there. It also stated that the camps *'will go on'* against military bases in this country, and to increase links with women's struggle to end oppression, prejudice, exploitation and violence throughout the world.

Later that evening some of the women went off to tell the other gates what we proposed to do, and after a huge curry supper, cooked mainly by Miranda and myself, a group of us sat round and continued the discussion. I have felt for a long time that Greenham

Common peace camps were more than just anti-cruise, and the women who go there are there for more than just that one reason. This time the discussion on oppression and class privilege among women were brought up again and again. Perhaps I just haven't been there before when these discussions took place, or is it that now there are so many women coming to Greenham from different backgrounds and countries that this sort of talk is more common and relevant? Women on social security also say that their lives at the camps are so much easier than women they know who have to struggle for everything even in this so-called welfare state that we live in. Some said that they were definitely better off and had far better and more luxury type food than they would have if they were at home. Life is easy, even with the cold, wet and lack of facilities. Those of us from privileged middleclass backgrounds had no idea how terrible real grinding poverty can be for women. Then the question of black and Asian women came up. A lot of those at the Orange Gate that night were from London and many belonged to women's groups there. They had tried at times to make contact with black and Asian women in their areas, but overall had not been very successful. Someone admitted that her group, quite without thinking, had suggested that two groups get together for a social evening, and said that the black and Asian women's group could do the catering for it! Not a popular suggestion and the evening ended up with white women only. This sort of unthinking mistake makes contact impossible.

Cleise said that she was on her own in Debbie's bender and I could put my things in there, as there was plenty of room. She did have the most awful cold, but as almost everyone I knew in Deal had flu, I decided a few more germs would not matter. Most of the residents were there including Margaret, Rebekah, Sian, Nikki, Ruth, Penny, etc., etc. and Miranda. I did confess to Miranda that I couldn't remember a word that she'd told me last time I was there when we went for a walk on the Common. I knew that she had been cross with me and that was all. She said that she could not remember a lot about it, except that she felt better for talking to me like that. Anyway, we laughed about it and decided that it did not matter. Sally was having a couple of week's holiday at home, and Diana was expected but was not there yet. I told them I had written up Diana's story about being arrested and they asked to hear it. I was very relieved that they enjoyed it, and told me that I must go on writing about the Orange Gate and happenings and stories as far as they knew, no one was doing it in quite this way.

We had some mulled wine, and two women offered to keep the night watch, as they said they were going off home the next day and could catch up on sleep then. This watch is long and boring, and uses up a lot of firewood, but we all feel it is necessary in case they try to deploy cruise during the hours of darkness. The instructions for the watchers are rather complicated, but the main thing is to be on the alert and rouse everyone.

In the morning, I decided that it was time I walked the perimeter fence. Nine miles is quite a long way and in the end *'waffle woman'* came. She got this name as she and her boyfriend had spent all day on the 11th serving free waffles to all who wanted them. Jan and I decided to go together and get to the Blue Gate at 2pm for the press conference. In the end, we did not leave until about 12, as we felt that a lunch/breakfast was the best sort of meal to have. Jan took some beer and sandwiches with her and we ate these while watching some soldiers make a new camp for themselves inside the fence. I don't think they like being looked at, but we doubtless have plenty of that to contend with. The first part between the Orange, Yellow and Green gates was very muddy and a lot of balancing on bits of wood, and generally sloshing along rather slowly. We only stopped briefly at the main gate. They have so many visitors and people; we did not intrude too much. We were very pleased at one point to find that for half a dozen panels or so, there was no fence up at all, just posts, and many soldiers inside the barbed wire. By the time we got to Green gate we needed a rest, and sat for a while by the fire and talked about the differences in the camps. There it is quiet and peaceful and I told them about the terrible noise at Orange with the soldiers shouting all the time and hurling stones at the benders to keep us awake. Green Gate has its problems too, the soldiers use loudspeakers to shout to keep them awake, and as the benders are very scattered, the odd empty one has been vandalised, but whether by the troops or vigilante groups no one is sure.

There seemed to be quite a lot of walking to the Turquoise Gate, but there were only a couple of tents there and we rather passed it without realising where we were, and soon after that we reached the Blue Gate. Lots of women were standing around after the press conference. Of course, we were rather too late for it, but we stayed and talked for a while and I saw some friends I had not seen for a while. I should mention that somewhere on our journey we met up with Rose, who was photographing and sketching as she went. She is a painter and told us she had hitchhiked down from Sheffield on her own the day before, something she had not done for years. We talked quite a bit about joining forces on a book and she was interested in the idea. Originally, I had wanted my son Mark to take photos for me, but he decided that, as a man he could not come to Greenham and it would be even worse if he started taking photos. Of course, he was quite right, but I had not thought of it in quite that way before he said it. By this time it was after 3, and we had only come half way, so Jan, Rose and I went on to the Indigo Gate where there was nothing at present, but talk of setting up a camp the next day.

At the Violet Gate, it was nice to meet Carola again, and so we stopped and had a coffee with her and then the tall Dutch women appeared. They had been making a bender over the road on the common, as the strip of ground by the fence is only a few yards wide. This time they had come by car with another Dutchwoman, and were planning to stay a while.

Then on to the Red Gate, where Jules was living. Women there were also in the process of making another bender, so the whole base is well surrounded. It is rather cold and bleak on this side of the airfield with the narrow winding road. I do think these gates will be evicted first, as there are not enough women to do much about security. I also think they could have trouble with local vandals. Although, generally it is the Main (Yellow) Gate that attracts most attention.

It was getting dark by this time, so we went on home to the Orange Gate. Rose came with us, and when we got there I found there was room in a bender for her if she wanted to stay, and there were plenty of sleeping bags and blankets around. Her stuff was back at the main gate, but she had a lot of walking to do that night to get there. I think we, all three, felt we had achieved something by the walk, and it certainly gave me a new perspective on the size of the airbase, and also on how much damage had been done to that fence. Most of the panels have been damaged, some only slightly, and some very severely indeed. There were practically no police on the outside, and the soldiers on the inside looked young, bored, and cold. Actually, it had been a magnificent day, almost like spring. The helicopters no longer fly around all day, which was perhaps the biggest relief of all. I should mention that during our entire walk we were escorted by at least one soldier on the inside. He had his walkie-talkie and accompanied us, reporting in when we stopped, and then we were sort of '*handed over*' to the next man on his beat.

During our hours away, more women has arrived and gone. The population changes all the time. Then a group came from another gate and said there were going to be slides and a talk at the Friends Meeting House in Newbury, and all who wanted to come were welcome. I decided to wait as I was expecting Liz and Hilary to turn up. Supper was organised, coffee and later on more mulled wine. I did not really feel cold at Greenham at all this time, but it was interesting to note that the London women were the ones less able to cope with the wind and cold air. The smoke round the campfire was as problematic as ever, but if you sit down low on the ground, it is not nearly so bad. The area round the fire now is well sheltered by windbreaks and they do help to keep the wind away, but the smoke tends to swirl around inside rather badly.

Hilary and Liz eventually turned up, and luckily, they had had supper on the way, as by this time there was none left. Hilary found the smoke almost impossible to bear as she had conjunctivitis, so they decided to sleep in their car that night. The women who had gone to the slide show came back and said that it had been very good indeed and the Meeting House had been packed out with a very appreciative crowd. I went off to bed quite soon with my '*hottie*' and Cleise, who by this time was swigging quantities of hot water and garlic and obviously feeling pretty rotten. There must have been a change of soldiers inside the fence, as this lot were much quieter, and early in the morning I heard one of them reading aloud the notices painted on the benders, and he paused when he came to the one that said, "Every Six Seconds a Child Dies". His companion made a remark a moment later about how we spelt '*wimmin*', but at least they did not shout and hurl stones at us.

We cleared up in the morning and then I tried to read a bit of Vanity Fair, but it is hard to concentrate with so much going on around. Cleise and Jan both wanted to catch the one o'clock coach and Gabrielle to do some shopping, so I agreed to take them to Thatcham and get some milk, bread etc., as the shops would be closed for a couple of days. On the whole, the people of Thatcham seem to accept Greenham women quite well, although I am still conscious of the wood smoke smell on me when I go into a warm shop. I made a phone call in a box with no door, and Gabrielle and I went back to the Gate.

Hilary was sitting in their car, her eyes still very painful, so the campfire was impossible as far as she was concerned. We talked for a while and had a beer, and then I decided it was well past lunchtime so went and got some food. At that moment, one of the tall Dutch women turned up and said that her friends had been arrested as they were helping to set up a new camp at the Indigo Gate and police were making arrests. We all leapt into cars and rushed over there. Two benders were being made on a very muddy patch of 'grass' verge, and a few women were standing around, but more and more arrived within minutes, and soon we were linking arms and singing, while from over the road members of the Newbury and Crookham Golf Club looked on in horror. I was very tempted to go over there and apply for membership, but I did not have my handicap certificate with me and under the circumstances, I do not think I would be very welcome! My handicap of 7 would be a good entry there, and all the women were longing for me to try. Perhaps another time I will.

Apart from building the benders, some women were digging a small ditch with pick and shovel in the awful stony ground. It appears that there is some bylaw that states that if a fence or ditch is joined up round a dwelling, it is much harder to evict, as the authorities have to get proper permission. It seems very odd. We were not sure how deep the ditch should be, and all we dug was a little gully about 6 or 9 inches deep. Never mind, there were so many women there, the police didn't want trouble with a crowd 50 or 60, so we went off after a while, although the decision to have the party at the Yellow Gate was altered to this new camp, so that it wouldn't be left too empty that first night.

Back at Orange Gate, we had another cup of coffee, and decided what to do that night. Margaret and I felt that we would rather stay where we were. We had to have a presence and watch at that Gate, and I am a law-abiding citizen who does not like to drink and drive. Anyway, a little action in our area would keep the security forces on their toes. Margaret said she had been for a walk to find out what the policy on arrests was and how many police were around, but she had not had much joy, and would I go and check. Well, I went off towards the Red Gate, and did not meet any police at all, and only the odd huddled soldier on the inside with his walkie-talkie at the ready. I stopped a few times, and fiddled with the fence, but no one came near me, so I reported back. I did not want to get arrested at that point and miss the party.

Food was being prepared, the wine was starting to flow, and many more *'regulars'* and newcomers had turned up. Zoe and her daughter greeted me in their normal polite way, and Diana's sister, Fiona, and their mother had come, so I was asked to read Diana's story to them and everyone. Diana was not well, but I gave them the copy of the story to give her when they went home, with my love. Francis from Northern Ireland and Jenny the actress, decided we hadn't got enough drink to last the evening, so we had a whip around and they came back quite soon with lots more wine, and also, they said for me, a bottle of Glenfiddich to see the new year in. My God, what a party! We all agreed it was different, much better than dressing up tidily and singing Auld Lang Syne, then not knowing what to do, or even worse, watching the never-ending TV trash.

Although it was still some way off midnight, Margaret thought that she and I ought to take another walk, so I collected my cutters, and off we went. About the only person we saw was a poor little soldier all on his own. He was terrified of us. If I had shouted "Boo" loudly, I think he would have run like hell. We asked him where he was from and he muttered Wales, so we told him we were sure that he would prefer to be home, and *would he like a cigarette?* He said he didn't smoke, so we did a bit more unravelling in front of him and went back to the fire.

Some women had gone off to Avebury to see the New Year in there, and some to the party at Indigo, but about 20 of us were left with the Glenfiddich and party spirit. At about midnight (give or take a minute or two) we rushed to the Gate, sang and danced, and of course I stood on my head, very conscious that the bolt cutters in my pocket were slipping rather rapidly towards the ground. I really must learn to behave in a more restrained way, but not yet, and certainly not at Greenham! Apart from other songs, we sang Auld Lang Syne, but the Greenham Women songs came over much better.

After a while Margaret, a few others, and I thought we ought to check that damn fence again, so strolled off in twos and threes. There was very little activity inside, so we did a little more damage, chatting all the while. We discussed what a lovely night it was, and the stars, and how nice it was to be in such good company etc., etc., but by this time we were all rather tired and a little drunk, so having wished the troops goodnight and a happy new year we went back to the campfire.

Hilary and Liz were going to drive home that night, and as Debbie, whose bender I had been sleeping in, was there, I had swapped places with Gabrielle, and there were three of us in a very small bender with a lot of things in it. Rose was already asleep when Jenny and I arrived, and we had to push her more to one side so we could get in with our *hotties*. I must say we were beautifully warm. In fact, Jenny told me she spent quite a lot of the night hurling off clothes. I woke with a bang at about quarter past nine, realised that Rose had gone, and that I had a tiny headache. I never get hangovers, so I thought this was unfair, but also I never sleep as late as that whatever time I go to bed, so I suppose it's all swings and roundabouts in this world. Jenny was going home very soon, so we got up and I had coffee and aspirin for breakfast, and very soon proper food, and felt fine. Rose greeted me with the news that she had got up at 8 and had taken a photo of me asleep in the bender. I thought this was very unfair. She said she would send me a copy. Thanks for nothing!

Everyone seemed happy but fairly subdued. We got the balloons and helium bottle out and I saw Penny making a mini bender. Her idea was to attach it to balloons and sent it off with messages of goodwill from Greenham Women. It seemed a lovely idea so I helped her, but with some doubt in my mind as to whether the weight would be too much for the balloons. Miranda cut out little cardboard Greenham Women and stuck them to the plastic top. Nikki made a lovely feminist symbol from rope and wool with a peace message to the woman who found it. We decided that as the strongish wind was from the south-west, we would carry it round the corner, towards yellow gate, so that at least for a while it would fly over the base. The police had been watching us make it and tying the balloons. They came and warned us that it would be hazard to traffic if it came down on a road. I said that they had more faith in its flying power than I had, but they said that *they were having bets on that*. Eventually about thirty of us carried it to the flying area. Jo, Penny and I with Rebekah and her washing bag taking the main strain. We realised that it was too heavy, and eventually with the aid of my penknife and lots of advice, cut away the wood and cardboard part and then to our relief and joy, and many photos, it sailed away beautifully and bravely over the fence and trees, gaining height all the time. It was a marvellous sight, and even the soldiers were delighted.

I had arranged with Jo and Gabrielle to leave at 4pm and give them a lift to London. I packed my things in the car and made sure that the bender was tidy and secure. I saw a good photo of Rebekah, Charlie and me taken last time I was there. I read an article in a Dublin magazine in which Margaret and I featured strongly. It dealt a lot with the wet and cold, Margaret's various activities and my energy and so-called efficiency. Oh well, fame at last.

Jo, another woman and I were very hungry, so we had some soup, then I saw Rebekah cutting meat, ham to be exact, and I couldn't resists a large chunk, then toasted cheese sandwiches, with the last of the fresh coffee. Three visitors were doing all the washing up, and then split big chunks of firewood for kindling, as the fireplace was totally clogged up. I talked to them for a while, then Jo, Gabrielle and I loaded up the car, said our goodbyes, and "see you again soon", and "take care", and left. My passengers slept quite a lot of the way to London, and in the three-hour journey, I had plenty of time to think and reflect on New Year's Eve and the coming of 1984. As we left it was starting to rain and blow, and I always have feelings of guilt leaving my friends to the bad weather when I am on my way to comfort. I would rather share the discomfort with them.

Incidentally, although I had all the makings for a bender for me a the Orange Gate, Nickie and others strongly advised Hilary, Liz and me not to make one at the moment, as under the new laws, they thought that all the benders could be pulled down and destroyed by the authorities. It was much better to keep the material until we all knew what was happening, so reluctantly I brought polythene, carpet, rope etc. home with me again.

January 1984: Deal, Kent

Back in this real, unreal world of home, life goes on. I meet old friends and acquaintances and the phone rings constantly. Friends can sometimes be a little unkind, or perhaps truthful. I am not sure which. The first woman I bumped into in the town when I was shopping, said hello quite quietly, then had a double take, and gushed forth how glad she was to see me as she had read in the paper that a Greenham woman had been arrested for being drunk and disorderly, and she had feared it might have been me! When I got home, the next three phone callers all said the same thing. I really do not really think my reputation calls for these sort of comments, I am not as bad as all that. I know I like to enjoy myself and even let my hair down on occasions, but I feel rather hurt that all these people have such unkind thoughts about me, hurts me to the core. Even my son made the same remark to me. Surely, he knows me better than that? I had heard about the arrest at another gate at Greenham when I was up there, and the actual incident was that a woman was trying singlehandedly to stop a police car from driving off by sitting on the bonnet. I am glad I wasn't around. I might have helped her.

One of the good things at the Orange Gate us the nice women you meet there. Round the campfire over the weekend I was talking to someone called Jo. I told her I came from Deal and she asked me if I knew a great friend of her parents who had moved to my part of the world and was a member of a golf club. Her name was Audrey. Well, of course I know Audrey. I have just resigned from being the handicap secretary of my club and Audrey had taken the job on. Believe it or not, but more or less the first phone call I had when I got back was from Audrey about a golf query. She is a very nice, extremely respectable Conservative (with a capital C) lady, and I do not think she even knew that I was one of those awful Greenham women, who she has seen and shuddered at on the tele. She knows that my politics are rather suspect, but on the whole it's not feasible to talk politics to anyone at the club, so I keep fairly quiet about my views, and never sell Labour Party raffle tickets at Christmas time, although Conservative ones are always being bought and sold. Jo had wanted me to say where we had met, so with some pleasure I told Audrey that I had been talking to this delightful young woman round the campfire at Greenham, at the New Year. There was a sort of deadly hush for a moment while Audrey recovered herself, then said faintly, "Oh how nice. I have not seen Jo for such a long time. I always liked her so much, but of course, I didn't know her all that well. My daughter was very friendly with her sister, but even all those years ago, the sisters weren't a bit alike."

I have seen Audrey a couple of times since that conversation, but somehow I do not think she views me in quite the same light now. I think I must have blotted my copybook and Jo's as well.

I have been wondering about joining the Newbury and Crookham Golf Club! It would be very convenient to have the odd game when I stay at the Orange Gate. If I applied for membership, it would make a good local address and with a handicap of 7, the members would have to find some really good excuse not to accept me. It would give my Greenham friends plenty of advantages, they could use the facilities, showers, loos etc., come and have a drink with me in the bar, and perhaps earn a bit of pocket money when times were hard, as caddies. One other use would be the odd sliced ball being knocked into the base. "Please can I have my ball back, mister?" Or, "I was only cutting a hole so I could get my ball out". We could have endless fun. In fact, I can see only two problems, one if that the subscription is probably rather high in that wealthy area of Berkshire, and the other is that I would be blackballed from every golf club in the country, and I do enjoy playing. I will have to give the idea a bit more thought and consideration.

20th – 22nd January 1984

I really had no intention of going to Greenham this weekend but I had phoned Waffle Jan the previous Monday. She told me that they were going to be very short of women, as lots of them were going to Holy Loch for a big demo, so the call was for as many regulars to turn up and hold the fort. OK, most plans can be changed, so I got myself organised and arranged to go with Hilary from Faversham. On Thursday evening, Hilary phoned me, saying she was feeling awful with a temperature and flu, so in the end I went on my own.

When I arrived at Orange Gate, at lunchtime, I really was glad that I had gone. Cleise, Margaret, Sally and Rebekah were the only women around. They made me welcome, especially when I produced a large saucepan of vegetable risotto ready cooked for supper! Once again, the gate and camp had changed. The previous week Newbury Council had engaged two men as bailiffs/wardens to clear the women off the Common. This means that nothing at all must be left around, except by the fence. No chairs, polythene wind breaks, wood for the fire, kitchen bender, and no tents. Nothing. Anything that is on the common when the bailiffs make their rounds will be taken away. One useful thing is that if we pile up the rubbish in sacks, they cart that away, which saves us a job. We did have a small fire in the clearing on the common, but all the food has to be carried over the road, and cups and kettles of water for tea and coffee, also have to be moved back and forth. The washing up and washing areas are now right by the fence, so the soldiers watch us from only a few feet away through the mesh. In some ways this does make communication and friendly chat with them easier. These particular Royal Irish Rangers from Northern Ireland were, on the whole, polite and pleasant. I was actually called "Ma'am" by a couple of them.

Cleise was busy sorting out the new kitchen bender. We had been chucked off the common in terrible weather. Everything had been rather thrown undercover, and as it was a lovely day, and very quiet, it seemed a good opportunity to get it all sorted out. The rats were being a damn nuisance. They were extremely bold; so all food has to be put in containers. Next evening we discussed the rats and Jill said she would bring some farm cats along to deal with them, as none of us would even contemplate using poison. If something was not done, the rats become even more of a health hazard.

I put my sleeping bags in Ruth's bender as she was away in Wales, and then helped with general tidying and sorting out of things round the camp. Just before dark Cleise and I went for a walk to warm up before the evening. As always, it is beautiful on the common, sombre shades of brown and green, and suddenly a brilliant tiny patch of orange fungi on a branch. Some of the trees are beginning to sprout buds, although it is only January, but to have pasted the shortest day and feel that spring must come, is an achievement.

We had an early supper and the five of us sat round talking and had a bottle of mulled wine later. This really does feel right for me, this place. With a blanket round my shoulders, a fire in front, and the friendship and companionship of these women, I do not feel the cold, although the ground is frozen hard, and I try to avoid too many trips to the shit pit. People back home talk about the hardship of the life there, and of course, it gets very tiring for the women who are there all the time. I don't think I could cope with it for too long, but when I am there, I'm totally at home, at ease, feel invigorated, and am part of something; the new revolution, anarchy, feminism, a different life style. We talk a lot about this, about ourselves, why we are there, and it is not just cruise missiles. Could we live together in such harmony without the tension of cruise, without the mud and cold and physical discomfort? It is hard to separate these things. *Is it the bad that makes it good?*

Anne turned up on her bike and Cleise, Sally and Rebekah drifted off to their benders. While Margaret, Anne and I stayed and talked for some time as although I knew however comfortable and warm, I would be in the bender, the first night away I never sleep that well.

The next morning was bright, cold and clear, idea camping weather! I decided to sort out the woodpile, which was in a muddle under polythene, but when I got down to it, I was appalled how little wood there was. We decided we might have to go into town, get a local paper, and perhaps buy some wood. Well miracles always happen at Greenham, as all day long women arrived with more wood, some pinched out of skips in London, some collected from the woods in other areas, and some actually bought for us. By the end of the day, once again we had a huge pile.

Old friends appeared. Marion had been keeping a vigil at Holloway for Anne, the vicar's wife. Unfortunately, Anne was not at Holloway, as it was full and no one knew quite where she was. We were all horrified at her sentence of 30 days, rather than the usual 7.

Marion also showed me the report of horrors done by the soldiers to the women since the bringing of cruise, which has been complied by Sian and Nikki. They included: having a spike being thrust through a bender, huge lumps of concrete being hurled at another one, masturbating in front of the women, peeing in the washing and washing up bowls, smearing toothbrushes with excrement and mud, the same on bedding, threats of gang rape, and the usual verbal abuse, which goes on most of the time. This report has been given to the press, and since then things seem to have improved. The women felt it depended very much on which regiment was patrolling the fence, and even more so on the officer in charge. Some positively encouraged harassment of the women at Greenham.

Liz arrived from Canterbury as arranged, but said that she was only going to stay for the day. Jill who was staying overnight, other familiar and new faces from London and Sheffield, and Maura from Tunbridge Wells turned up. We had heard that the police and soldiers expected some sort of action that day. They had heard that many women were going to be there, and as the day wore on, Margaret felt that we should not disappoint the authorities, but have a little party. I agreed with her and so did Maura. Most of the others had court cases coming up or commitments of some sort, but said that they would gladly cause a diversion.

Rebekah had gone back to London in the morning, and later on in the day after Cleis, Liz and I had had a walk, Cleis felt that she wanted to go back, so I took her to Thatcham and on my way home, did the round of the Gates on the north side. It was amazing. The day before, these gates had practically no one there but by the early evening women were arriving every few minutes. I had wondered if these gates, Blue, Indigo and Red would have enough women to hold them, but my fears were groundless. Some women offered to do night watch while other slept, and the general feeling of goodwill and companionship was all round the fence. Is it telepathy, or phone calls, which bring these women at a time of need on a bitterly cold January night? I think a bit of both.

Back at Orange, supper had been prepared, the corks drawn, and those who could sing started singing. Actually, that is not quite true; everyone sang who knew the words of Greenham songs. I heard that someone is going to compile a tape of songs, and I would certainly like to have it. We then decided to sing to the soldiers by the fence, so a mass exodus from the fire took place, and those of us prepared to cut the fence, put bolt cutters in our pockets and joined them. Everyone sang like mad and tried to get the soldiers to join in with us and there was quite a lot of friendly talk. I should mention that some time earlier women had put Super Glue in the padlock on the gate, so we knew that would cause confusion when it was discovered. Soon Margaret, Maura and I drifted off back to the campfire and then through the undergrowth towards the main gate. We could see in the arc lights, soldiers huddled near their braziers, which were about 100 yards apart. We walked down near some trees for cover and started cutting, but almost instantly there was a slight commotion inside, so the three of us made a hasty retreat onto the common, where we sat quietly and had a little think. We decided that we had been too close to a tent on the corner where there were reinforcements, so we would go back near the benders and singers and just snip and do a bit of damage. Well, we walked up to the fence right in front of a soldier and started cutting. He just watched us. We snipped from overhead height down to the ground and then I stepped inside and cut the coiled barbed wire. The soldier could not believe it. I am not sure whether he was reporting in on his walkie-talkie, but Maura was all the time talking to him in her lovely Irish voice saying that his ancestors would be ashamed of what he was doing etc., etc., and so we went on snipping. Eventually when I was standing right inside the fence, he leaned forward to take my cutters from me and said rather weakly, "Don't cut anymore". So I backed out, and Margaret and I returned to the singers, leaving Maura arguing with him. Margaret said that she felt it was a private argument between the Irish, and it was better if we left them to it (the next morning Maura said she could not remember arguing with him, but was just rather surprised to find we had gone).

Back at the benders, I went up to Liz and swapped her balaclava for my woolly hat, and we just all went on singing happily. Margaret went straight to her car and to bed. She said that she was sure the police would recognise her, so she would pretend to be asleep. Maura put on her shawl-like scarf again, and after a while we all drifted back to the campfire. Before long, the MoD police arrived with the soldier who had watched us cutting. He was obviously told to identify the ones who had done the terrible deed but he shook his head, having looked hard at both Maura and me, and they went off, to shouts and laughter from us.

After I had gone to my bender where I slept soundly, Maura and some of the others talked to the soldiers again, and listened to a song that the soldiers were making up about us. I cannot remember it all, but it went something like this:

As we were standing guard at Greenham at midnight,
Some women came along and cut the fence by candlelight.

I hope by now, they have put some more words to it, as we all thought it was very nice.

Early next morning some of the women from Sheffield had been highly amused to hear two soldiers talking about the previous night:

"I don't know what's wrong with the 'effing padlock on the gate. It won't work it's all stuck up. The women did it."

"I hear that the women cut the wire last night. What was it? Just a little hole?"

"Little? *It was fucking enormous!*"

One story I heard on Sunday was when the practice alert went a few days earlier for the Americans and families to get into their bunkers, they came streaming along in their cars with wives and children in pyjamas, while the whole of Newbury was in a flap over the alarms. It took about two hours before all the personnel were inside the camp, by this time some of the troops had been issued with rubber suits, helmets and guns (presumably to control their fellow Americans and possible any British who might want a place in the shelters as well). At a certain time, these men went round, telling their comrades that they were dead, and then they raised a black flag over the camp. We have been telling as many of the British troops as possible about this, as the present technique of changing the regiment every week means that the new men will not hear about it. The women said it really was a pathetic sight.

More visitors with food and mainly wood, also came on Sunday. Di arrived with her mother, children and a friend. She had just spent a week in Holloway where one of her duties had been to pack war games toys, she and another Greenham woman objected, and they were put in solitary. Di had to stay there for 28 hours, but she said it was worth it, as in the end she saw the Governor and the rule has been changed that if for reasons of conscience a woman won't do a job like that, she will be given alternative work sewing. Di took my name, address and phone number, as it appears that quite soon there is going to be an all-women's action in my area, and of course, I can help quite a bit.

Pat Arrowsmith also paid us a visit. She is someone I have heard about since the early Aldermaston days and it was nice to meet her. The one thing she disapproves of about Greenham women is that when they are put in prison, they don't try to escape! She really is an expert on this, and I told her I knew a friend of hers from Deal, Bruce, who told me a story how when they were both working for Amnesty some years ago, she had turned up, and they had gone to a restaurant for a meal. And how horrified he had been, when he realised she was on the run!

During the day news trickled in from the other Gates about action that had taken place on Saturday night. At the Yellow Gate, 5 or 6 women had been arrested, and at the Blue, the soldiers had been very rough and unpleasant with women there, and had made them lie on the ground, spread-eagled for a long time, and had been vocal and nasty. We were really very lucky to have got away with it again at Orange. I am beginning to think I lead a charmed life.

I had been feeling very worried about the permanent residents who by this time were down to two, Sally and Margaret. They were both exhausted, mentally more than physically, and needed a break. I had a word with Jill and Anne and we agreed that I would take Sally back with me for a few days for a holiday, and they would take it in turns to cover a night with Margaret, as they both live quite locally, but work during the day. Then Hester said that she was going to stay for a few days, and that Zoë was coming that night, and the Sheffield women said that they also could manage at least a couple of nights. Anyway, between us, we persuaded Sally to come with me, and Margaret thought it an excellent idea and said that she would have a break quite soon herself. We also knew that Shirley, Sian, Kim and others would be back from Holy Loch as soon as they could, but the weather up there had been so awful that they might be delayed for a while. Anyway, there were enough women to cover for a few days, and no one person is indispensable. That is what Sally firmly told herself and she went off to get her things.

While she was doing this I did a bit of washing up, and the Ranger said "good day" politely, then "You're skivvy today are you?" I explained that we did not have duty rotas, if we saw some job needed doing, and we were happy to do, we just got on and did it. Nobody told or even asked someone else to do a job, we didn't need to. He nodded in agreement politely, but I don't think he really believed me. Men don't function that way. They organise and everyone has a duty. I don't think anarchy would work with men, but it certainly seems to with the women at Greenham.

Sally and I left at about 3 o'clock, as there was a terrible forecast. This time I did not leave Greenham as soon. As I drove away from the Orange Gate, I took a bit of Greenham home with me.

I think Sally appreciated the break. A hot bath on Sunday night, a drink then bed. On Monday, it poured with rain for hours, blew and was foul. When I came back from work, it was getting better and I took Sally to see the sea. As we walked on the pier the clouds lifted, yellow light flooded the town and it really looked beautiful. We then went and saw Hilary, who asked us to supper the following evening. I took Sally up to Kingsdown where we saw the lights shining in France, on to Olivia's for tea, then home and supper. The next day I went to work as usual, and during the morning Sally went down the road to Olivia's to talk astrology. I arranged that she would come with Hilary and me to the WEA class in Dover, which was on *Women and Peace*, so the two-hour session was really discussion and questions and answers on what makes Greenham women tick. Then a meal and drink back at Hilary's, then home and bed. Sally had decided that she wanted to go back on Wednesday, so in the morning we drove through Sandwich to Canterbury and inspected the Cathedral. She got a coach at 1 o'clock. When I see this written down, I don't think it can have been much of a rest for Sally, but it certainly was a change. I know I enjoyed having her, and will try to bring other residents when I come home again.

4th February 1984

I always like to take visitors to Dover Castle for a visit, but this time it was a bit different. We did not go inside the castle to see the armour, or throw pennies down the well; we went to see if we could find a good way to break into the underground bunker, or Regional Seat of Government, as it used to be called.

Originally, there were going to be five or six women coming at 11am, but in the end only two arrived at 1pm. Having met in Deal in the most conservative coffee bar I know, we came back to my house, grabbed a sandwich and went over to Dover in the hire car, with no stickers anywhere in sight. Di actually donned a headscarf, and apart from Blue's nose stud and my rather dirty jeans, we were a trio of utmost respectability.

I showed them where the coaches parked so their visitors walked into the castle grounds, and then we drove through the very narrow car entrance past the traffic signals. They agreed that there was no way a coach could get near, but minibuses would be fine. We parked the car in the official car park then walked back to the main entrance of the bunker. They were both very intrigued by the bell and spy hole in the door, but thought it might be tempting fate too much to ring the bell. There was a newly cemented manhole cover by the entrance, but we felt that would be too difficult to move, so we walked all-round the area, paying special attention to the large abandoned building quite close. Most of the windows were broken or nailed up with Perspex or wood, and when we had gone right round it, we found that quite a lot of the below ground level doors and windows were completely missing. It meant climbing over a spiked fence to get down to that area, but without doubt it could easily be done. I felt that here might be a trap door from there leading towards the bunker, but in the end we decided that it was so easy to get into, by children or anyone, that it was not really worth going down there at that time. Just as we had completed our circuit of the building, we saw a custodian in uniform coming towards us, carrying a large red torch (a torch in broad daylight!) We strolled towards the high bank where we could see over the cliff edge, and I gave a loud lecture on Shakespeare Cliff, and the glories of Dover Harbour. That was the first person we had seen since our arrival, but as it was a very dull and damp day, it was not surprising.

I do not know if the guard was taken in by my discourse, but he just looked hard at us as he went past, and we clambered up a man-made mound to have another look round. A moment later, Blue called Di and me, and said that she had found an entrance in the mound under where we were standing. It had been blocked-off by breezeblocks, but the top couple of rows had been broken and knocked out, and there was a hole, just big enough to crawl through, about five feet above the ground. I got my torch out, stood on the broken breezeblocks, and looked in. I could not see a lot, but in the gloom, there appeared to be a brick staircase leading down, in the direction of the bunker entrance, which was only about a hundred yards away. We could not really be seen by anyone, as there was a short path leading to this entrance, so Di said she wanted to have a look for herself. She clambered up, and I hitched her up a bit higher. When she came down, we discussed what we had seen, and she said she wanted to take her skirt off and go in there in her tights. Just as she was saying this, we heard a noise that sounded like a cough, it was leaves rustling in the wind, but to be on the safe side, we walked back up the path, and as we did so, we heard the sound of what Di positively identified as keys rattling. Di had just spent a week in Holloway, so she was the expert on that. We beat a very hasty retreat up the road, (actually running like hell for a few yards), then slowed down, and I looked back. There was a young man walking away from the little path, wearing a light blue tee shirt and dark trousers, carrying a jacket, brushing dirt off his shoulders: Without doubt, the only place he could have come from was the hole in the breezeblocks.

Di, Blue and I just kept walking away. Who was he? If he had been a workman, and this was a Saturday afternoon, he wouldn't have been in such a hurry to get away from us. Had he heard what we had been saying? There were many places in the area that would have made a far easier squat, the abandoned building for example. We made our way back to the car, and then I went off on my own, to see if I could see him, but he had obviously gone off down the road away from the castle. I came back and we sat and talked for a while. Had we been pre-empted? The mystery remains. Apart from anything else, we felt awful fools. Enid Blyton and the adventurous five (or three) had nothing on us!

I had been told that some boys had climbed into the bunker sometime previously from above the terrace, so we drove round there and looked up. There was a blue air vent coming out from the white cliffs quite high up, and a bit of blue building near it. We could not see how to get very close, and then I wondered about the talk about other entrances tunnels under the cliffs and the new coastguard station. We drove round that way, but realised that it is really quite a long way from there to the bunker site. As, there were masses of tunnels and hollowed out chambers in the, cliffs, we decided to walk back along the footpath under Jubilee Way and see if we could see anything like the pipe that Di had been told about, coming down onto the beach. We passed right under the, air vent, and agreed that it would be quite possible to climb up the steep but grassy hill to it, and over the fence. That would be no problem, but obviously, it must be done at night. Di and Blue said they would have to come back in a few weeks' time, and try then, and I could do the driving and wait for them. This seems our best hope, but just to check this was the pipe that Di mentioned, we went on down to the beach, and as I thought could not see any sign of anything like that. Blue took a photo of the blue air vent, pretending that she was taking a picture of us, draped tastefully on a boat. But, as it was very dusky by that time, I doubt if she will get much out of it.

We walked back to the car, and drove home. Di and Blue had to get back that night, so we had supper, and arranged to find out more, and meet at Greenham on the 16th 'Feb. Di informed me to be careful about making contact with her, as without doubt her phone was tapped, and also some mail was opened. It is a very odd world I am living in, and certainly, that was not the usual *visitors-to-Dover* type of trip.

16th -18th February 1984

I stayed with Hilary in Faversham overnight, so got an early start to Greenham, and was in time to see Shirley before she left the Orange Gate for America, having stayed there for three months. She was wearing a splendid coat made from blue blankets, with bright patch pockets and trimmings and hand carved toggles. Rebekah and Charlie were going with her to Gatwick, and then on to Lyndon, so I had their bender. I think it was the nicest one I have slept in, beautifully warm and dry, and lots of decorations and personality. I was very comfortable. Anne Francis was there having spent three weeks in Holloway, Sally, Sian, Isla, Liz, another Shirley, a woman whose name I never got, and two women who had walked round from the Blue Gate. We agreed that the bean and vegetable casserole I had made would be plenty with just a bit of rice to go with it, so there was no cooking to do that night. I was introduced to the new resident, Timothy, who is black and white, with one ragged ear, but he has decided that without doubt he prefers sitting on laps and sleeping in Sian's bender, to catching rats. Jill did explain to me, in his defence, that if you point him in the right direction he does run after the rat, but I don't think he has caught one yet (or ever will). When we sit round the campfire in a tight circle, Tim walks from knee to knee until he finds the right lap and settles down. There is a great deal of competition to have him, and not just for the warmth he generates. He is a lovely cat. Jill also says that since he has come, the level of intelligent conversation has definitely gone down!

We sat and talked, made coffee and toast, then most of the women wandered off, and I was left to greet Phil Thomas and the ten Donnington students and give them a grand tour of the Orange Gate. I took them down the fence to the swamp, showed them the benders, and talked to them and answered questions for about two hours. We ended up round the campfire with cups of coffee, and I think some of them will certainly come back to Greenham again. After they had gone, I found I was in sole-charge of the Orange Gate, no one else around at all, so I did some washing up and tidied up a bit, and had a spot of trouble with Danny, Tommy and John from the caravans up the road. In the end, I gave them some sweets, and then hid the rest. I also hid some fireworks in my car, which they were about to pull to pieces. The next day they behaved even worse. They stole food from the kitchen bender, poured a large jar of oats all over the road, and cycled over them. Last time I had been there, they had thrown eggs at my car, and hurled oranges about, but this time we all felt that this destruction of food was too much, so Sally and Sian went and saw their parents. I am afraid they will get a beating. They really were making life impossible for the women.

Ann and I thought it was time we dug a new shit pit, so went off with pick and spade. The ground is hard and stony, but we managed to make quite a deep pit, and then I took some of the soil in a box for Barbara in London to plant her new rose that she has ordered, called Greenpeace It seems very appropriate to plant such a rose, with Greenham soil round its roots.

The women who had been away during the day came back, and Jill and Ann from Reading arrived. We had a meal with some wine and beer, and sat and talked round the fire until quite late. Then I. crawled into the bender with my *hottie*. I went to sleep quickly and slept soundly, having had only about three hours sleep the night before. The air was very cold to breathe, as there was a very hard frost, but I kept my ears pretty well covered, so was not worried by the noise of the soldiers shouting, and the usual traffic in the base.

Friday was court day. I had promised Sally that I would take her to the magistrate's court with Ann and Judy, and watch the proceedings. We parked the car in Newbury, had a coffee, and walked to the court. There were not so many women there as last time I had been, but these cases were all going to take much longer and were more complicated. Isla and I got seats in Court 1, and watched Chris, Steph and Philippa defending themselves. There were on a charge of blocking the road to traffic at the Blue Gate back in November, and their defence was that they had not been blockading, but dancing across the road, when they were suddenly arrested. The police maintained that the women had stopped a car coming out of the gate, and that they had been given a warning before they were arrested. For reasons known only to himself, the stipendiary magistrate let Philippa off, but fined Chris and Steph £10 and £5 costs. I believe for an identical offence later, he let Booan and Liz off. All very odd.

The case against Ann, Judy and Sally was very complex. They were all arrested for fence cutting the day after the big demo on 29th Oct. Ann particularly felt it was a 'grudge' arrest as she had made a complaint about one of the policemen only the week before. Anyway, the three women went for a walk along the fence quite late at night and were pulling at the fence as it was in a hell of a state, having been chopped by about two thousand women the previous day. They saw the headlights of a vehicle inside, so Judy sat down and the other two strolled off. Almost instantly police came along and arrested them, and took them to Newbury nick. The RAF police gave evidence. The first one said that he was in the back of the Land Rover and saw the three women cutting the fence in the lights of the vehicle, and the one in the purple poncho (Judy) who had done the cutting passed something to another woman, and then sat down on the ground. The prosecuting lawyer asked him a lot of questions, and then the women had their turn. They asked many questions, mainly about the actual cutting, how many snips taken had the RAF man seen, what angle was the Land Rover to them and the fence, how big were the cutters, which hand had Judy held them in, could he see them being passed, etc. The most telling point was that he insisted that Judy had cut with her right hand only, and of course, the wire is too thick to use only one hand. Also he could not swear (ha ha) whether she had taken two or three cuts. In the end, the questioning was finished, and the three magistrates decided to break for lunch. They warned the man not to talk about it to his colleague, but he went straight out of the court to have lunch with him, and Isia followed and heard him say, "Don't say anything now, that woman is listening to us." Hester who was waiting outside the court also heard this, but by the time Anne Judy and Sally joined us, Hester had gone, and we needed her to be a witness for the women. Isia could not do this as she had been in the courtroom. Panic stations all round. The three defendants go off to have lunch and Isia and I charged round Newbury to try to find Hester. In the end, I told Isia to keep looking, and I rushed round in the car to all the gates in case she had turned up there. No sign of her at all, and I just got back to the court before it started, and Hester was there!

Ann straight away tried to get the case dismissed, but was told that at that point in the proceedings it was impossible. The second RAF witness was brought in and he was even more unpleasant than the first. He was asked on oath whether the case had been discussed over lunch and said that it had not and then proceeded to read out the statement, which he had written up at the time of the arrest. He said more or less the same as the first bloke and there was a lot more questioning about the actual cutting, but the same unsatisfactory answers were given. It really was like trying to wade through thick cotton wool.

The first policeman called was the one who had arrested Ann, and had also been accused by her on a previous occasion of behaving incorrectly. He was of course asked if this had affected his judgement of her, but he denied this with a look of complete innocence and horror on his face. As with the RAF men, Ann and the others were allowed to read the statements and question the officers about things in them. The point that Ann picked up was the fact that although he stated that when he arrested her she had a piece of wire about a foot long in her hand, he didn't take this from her as evidence, but produced a couple of little pieces which he had found in the van on the way back to Newbury. It seemed to me in the main that Judy was the woman they were really after. They kept saying that she was the one who had done the cutting. She asked her arresting officer where he had arrested her, and kept saying that she hadn't done it. The whole fence was cut anyway, so how could they possibly know which hole had been cut at which time? Also, they all said that if they *had* cut the fence, they would be happy to admit it. Sally's officer said that he thought she was being uncooperative and this upset her, quite rightly so. They were all under a tremendous strain. Then when the prosecution witnesses had finished, Ann was allowed to say that she thought the case should be dismissed, and the three magistrates went off to have their huddle. When they came back, they said that they were not prepared to do this, and as it was getting late, 4 o'clock, the case would be adjourned until Tuesday. We were all shattered at this, and left the court feeling very depressed. Anne with the patchwork jeans, had her bike to go home on, but I was not prepared to take women home in my car so Hester and Pat said they would get a bus to the main gate and I would pick them up from there at about 4 o'clock.

Isia and I did some shopping, mainly food for Timothy, and we went back to Orange Gate. I was glad that I had some wine, which Phil and the students had given us, as we all needed a drink. We had bought Guinness for Sally, and we started on that on the way home in the car. It was all so unsatisfactory being left in the air like that. The three women were all very subdued, but Sally and Judy decided to go to London the next day and I said I would take them in the car.

We had the usual good evening. Pat, who is the woman who had been sacked by Leeds Council then reinstated, was telling us about this and other arrests, Shirley about a visit from Naomi Mitchison to the Yellow Gate some time previously, and general chat. Camilla arrived, and told me that she had an excellent colour slide of me standing on my hands against the Orange Gate on New Year's Eve, which she was showing to various groups around the country: *fame at last*! Then the night watch turned up from Guildford. They come every Friday night, and just sit up and relieve all the tension of being overnight at Orange Gate. Jo arrived from Glasgow, and by this time I had collected Hester and Pat, and Jill and Ann came back again. Sally was feeling very low and let down, so she went off to her bender early, but the rest of us stayed up for ages, and in the end let off the fireworks that I had hidden in my car. Just to check, I stood on my hands. In fact, I think I can do it better when I'm drunk rather than sober. Actually, I was not that drunk, just a little merry. A new batch of soldiers had arrived that day, so were very quiet and well behaved. The previous lot, as usual, had been offensive on their last night, so Friday is always treated as being a good night by the women. I did feel that we should have done a little carnage to the nice new bit of fence, which was being put up near the gate, but in the end we decided to leave it for another day, or night.

One interesting thing did happen that evening. A police van drew up, and we all went rather stiff. The sergeant said that there was an odd man, a peeping tom, on the prowl, and he was warning us to be on our guard, and if we did see someone like that around, to tell them at the gate, and the information would be put through to the civil police. It appeared that Jo had come on the coach with him, and as able to give a good description of the man, but we certainly had not seen him round our gate that night.

Another beautiful, clear, cold night. Greenham would be fantastic without the American Air base and Cruise missiles, but where would we all be? I slept soundly and was up in good time to take Sally, Judy, the Greenham soil and myself to London.

1ˢᵗ – 5ᵗʰ March 1984

It is not hard to balls up the most perfectly laid plans, and this is what happened to my early morning start to Greenham. Staying with Hilary in Faversham cuts down mileage and time, in theory, but not always in practice. Actually, she forgot I was coming, O.K. but then her car would not start in the morning so I gave her a lift into Canterbury, which was going completely backwards before I started forwards. All right. No real hassle, I arrived at the Orange Gate at 11.30pm.

For a bit, I'm the outsider. There were eleven Swedish women there, all lovely, nice, etc., etc., but they did not know me, and I did not know them. To be fair, the more I heard about them, the nicer they became. They did most of the work, were, supportive, kind, lovely, but there was a sort of language barrier, and when nine of them climbed into their vehicle, I did have a sense of relief. I also feel that if I had been there earlier, we could have got to know each other.

Sally was there, Sian, who quite soon went to London for a few days, Kay, Marion, Marta, Margaret, Eve, Natasha from NZ and two Welshwomen. The supper I had taken of chilli con carne was fine for that number. I distributed the vegetables from Thanet round the gates during the next afternoon, as Kay had to sign-on in Newbury. Sally came for the ride. It was a lovely day, spring was in the air, and I felt very optimistic about the future and the present, and meeting and greeting my friends again. Violet, and then Marion came back to Orange, and then Anne from Reading. I was home again without doubt.

Sometime during the evening, a woman came round from another gate with a present of some special flares for us. It appears that these that been pinched on a raid into a bunker from somewhere. The woman told us to be careful of them, showed us how they worked, and demonstrated that the paper covering had a piece of string attached, and if the string was broken, the flare would go off. Well, Sally put the two flares carefully in her bender, and we hoped that the other gates had been as careful.

I did not go to bed that early, although Marion and I had come to an agreement that we would do a night watch with E, and she would do the first one, and then wake me. I was in Miranda's bender, which was lovely, high, peaceful, but a little Spartan, with the bed area on planks, covered with just a couple of blankets, not the softest thing in the world to sleep on, but the bender was warm and dry. I left the campfire at about 11 pm, but frankly didn't sleep that well. The soldiers were on their last night, therefore were noisy, and anyway it takes a while to get used to Greenham type sleeping

Eventually I dropped off, having been brave enough to take off my trousers and two sweaters, and was aware of a lot of talking, over the intercom, as well as just outside the bender in the road, with flashing car lights. I took my ear outside sleeping bag and listened. The voices were American and English police and army, and in effect what had happened was that, at the gate, someone had seen the flares, pulled them apart, the string had broken, and the 'object' had started ticking in an ominous way. One of the women had told the MoD cops about this, and all hell had been let loose. From what I could hear from my bender, these flares should be dropped from planes. Once the string had been broken, they could take up to three hours before they went off, and they were filled with phosphorus, and therefore extremely dangerous up to an area of 45 feet away.

I decided it was time I got up when I heard that, as I was much closer than forty-five feet, and I felt very lonely and vulnerable on my own. I struggled back into all my clothes (that will teach me to take my trousers off at night at Greenham!) and went to the campfire.

Sally, Anne, Marion and the night watch were there, plus the police being rather officious, so Sally, Anne and I decided the best and safest thing was for the three of us to go round the other gates and warn the women there what was happening, rather than have the police go round, snooping and disturbing.

At Yellow Gate, they also had tried out one of the flares, and when it did not go off, the women chucked it in the gorse bushes. Luckily, these flares must have been old and dud, as no one had been hurt. It was hard to find anyone who knew what was happening, as the night watch women had no idea, and it is hard to wake up bender inhabitants. We did succeed and in the end went from the Yellow to the Green, to the Blue, Indigo-Violet and back home again. A nice little drive at 2.30am. We decided that Marion and I could go to bed, but it did not seem very long before Edna was calling outside my bender, that she had to go and could not wake anyone except me, so *"could I get up and keep an eye on things?"* Mind you, Anne had already gone off to work. So, I sat by the fire and had lots of cups of coffee before Margaret appeared briefly before her day off to Quaker friends in Newbury.

The wind was blowing cold and hard from the North West. It was going to be a long cold, hard day. I had time to think about how Sally, Anne and Judy had been found not guilty the previous week at the magistrates court. Sally told me that she could not believe it herself. They had arrived in the court with lots of supporters, including Ruth who had a huge piece of fence, almost like chainmail, round her neck, and clanked as she moved. The other women also pieces of fence in clear view, and one woman had her baby with her. She was told to take the baby out of the court, so all the women took turns in caring for the child on the landing, and when it was Ruth's turn, she carefully put her piece of chainmail round another woman's neck.

Anne, Sally and Judy gave their evidence in defence of themselves, and the magistrates deliberated for at least half an hour. When they came back and found them *"not guilty"* the three could not believe it. The only woman who took it in straight away was 'clanking' Ruth! If all was well and in this instance justice was done.

Friday was a day of doing things, and trying to keep warm in that biting wind. A new batch of soldiers took over, Coldstream Guards who proudly informed us that they had just been doing guard duty at Buckingham Palace. Bully for them. I hope they did not yell at the Queen at the tops of their voices *"cunt"* or *"this is a four minute warning, the Russians have just launched their missiles"*. She mightn't have liked it any more than I did.

Marta left for somewhere, and Isia arrived with Lucy, her little black cat. We now have four cats at the Orange Gate. Tim is of course the first feline resident, beloved by all, but Margaret has brought her two cats that are really very good rat catchers, which, is just what we want.

Visitors came and went. One brought a bottle of vodka, a man brought a load of wood from Gloucester, and I decided that I quiet kip would be nice, except that when I went into the bender, the wind was blowing so much, that I felt like I should be holding the whole structure down, as it was creaking. Actually, it is incredibly strong, and as I sit writing this, I fear that those bailiffs and bulldozers may have done, or are doing, what the gale could not. We will build better and stronger if necessary. Greenham women are a bit like their benders. They may sway a bit in the wind, but they will stand up to anything, and come back again and again.

Sleep was impossible so I went back to the campfire. E joined me with the bottle of donated vodka and orange juice. I told her that we shared donations, and did not start drinking them in the middle of the afternoon. She agreed quite readily, but we will have problems with *"that young woman"* who is in a special school, which she has run away from to come to Greenham. She has already gone round the gates, looking for something – who knows what – and playing a tape recorder far too loudly for the comfort of most of the women.

Sally asked me to come for a walk with her and showed me the hidden bender on the common. This will keep four or five women in secrecy and comfort when they are evicted from the benders by the fence.

What has happened is that Newbury Council, Berkshire County Council and the MoD have all got together so they can evict from anywhere round the base and will not tread on each other's toes. Actually, I am amazed they did not do this, ages ago. We still have the bailiffs coming to Orange once or twice a day and they take away our rubbish, which we put in bags and leave out on the common for them. The hidden bender is lovely, and then Sally showed me another place where she thought we could build one, and I suggested that if we propped up a fallen silver birch with another fallen tree at the forked piece, we could build round and under and it could easily be hidden. We said we would have a go the next day, then on our way back to camp we saw Marion wielding a pick for a new shit pit, so we helped her, plus great howls of laughter. The super refinement we added was carefully cut posts with loo rolls on top, covered with plastic bags to keep the paper dry. The paper can be pulled and unrolled without taking the bags off. My God, the ingenuity of women at Greenham!

It was still blowing like hell, but the snow flurries had stopped by this time, and Marion and I carried across our magnificent vegetable stew, which we had prepared earlier. It is impossible to guess how many women will be around for supper, as at weekends women just turn up, which is great. We hoped that our night watch women from Guildford would come as usual, and they did. This is one of the most dedicated tasks. Just sitting up round a campfire in a howling gale or rain, just to make sure that *'they'* do not try to take out the cruise convoys while we are all asleep.

As soon as its light, these women clear up the chaos of the previous night's supper and booze from the fire, wash up, and the

Guildford ones even do a water run, before going back home to their own lives. They do not get publicity as Greenham women and they should. I suppose the media would find them too respectable, clean & ordinary!

We sat, and talked round the fire. Margaret came back from her day off, and we had a little singsong. E got her vodka & orange, Isia had too much on an empty stomach, and the rest of us just got quite merry. I was going to do a bit of fence cutting, but the evening didn't seem quite right. You have to do these things at exactly the right time: biorhythms or instinct will tell you when.

I did not think the wind was quite so strong that night, and I slept quite well. Marion moved her van a little, as she thought it was going to blow over. The wind must have been at just the wrong angle.

Saturday was another day of coming and going. I was going to go shopping in the car, but somehow there was never enough time to get round to it. M told me that she told me that she had had to act as a 'mother figure' to young E the night before, as the kid was in a state, and wanted to talk. M said that she had stayed in the bender with her, and had tried to sort out her problems.

Anne came during the morning, and at about lunchtime, Sally, Anne and I decided it was time to make a start on the new bender on the common. We took a saw, rope, and some green bender making material off with us. I spent some time there, as these jobs should not be rushed, but also have to be hidden all the time. At one point I managed to gash my thumb, and went back to get a plaster, and there was Cleis. Nobody had seen her since I had taken her to Thatcham a month before, but she has been sorting out her life, and is now living in a women's cooperative in London. It was good to see her again, so she came with me, and we talked with Marion who was practising (with a lot of interruptions) her accordion on an out of the way path. We went on to the bender and did some more work on it, tying it down and covering it with gorse, etc.

We were rather perturbed to see two strangers gathering wood on the common, and Cleis, Marion and I decided to find out who they were. I had seen two vast mobile homes on lorry bases parked not far from us, so we went along there. The first thing we saw as we approached, were half a dozen bantams coming out of their home, down a ramp at the bottom of one van! Terry and Dominique introduced themselves and asked us in. They live in luxury, but they assured us, everything they had and ate, came out of dustbins. They travel all the time, Dominique mainly in the mountains in Provence, and Terry, wherever the whim takes him. He described himself as an aged hippy, and he certainly had the right length red hair and beard. We talked to them for ages, and so in the end asked Dominique to the campfire for supper with us. Their lifestyle is happy and free, and they seemed contented, peaceful and assured. It makes you wonder why people live in houses with tellies and all mod cons. Terry and Dominique had made all the bodywork on the two vans. They had one each, as they didn't always want to go to the same places at the same time. They did their scavenging on bikes, which they kept tied to the back of their vans. Terry said that he spent quite a lot of time cleaning up the area that he was parked in, so that on the whole the councils accepted him on their ground.

Back at the camp there was a feeling of tension around, and Isia told us what had happened. E had been talking to her, and she maintained that M had been rather more than just motherly to her, and was very upset and wanted to leave. Oh God, that's all we want in the way of problems. Cruise, wind, soldiers, cold, etc., paled into insignificance compared with this. We all know that M, to put it mildly, is in a bad mental state at present, while E admits she is in care at a special school. There was no sign of M that evening; she had gone off to bed early, and the Swedish women said that E could stay in their bender with them, as it was not a good thing for her to be on her own. We decided to leave this problem until the next day.

Sunday was mild, soft and damp, more like autumn than spring, with uncovered hair changing colour as the tiny rain drops built up. Kay, Isla and I decided to go shopping in Thatcham for milk and staples, as no one had got anything for a couple of days. I really think our most important item was cat's food! The people of Thatcham seem to accept us quite well, and although we are occasionally stared at, there is no abuse. We were not there long.

By the time we got back to Orange Gate, the visitors were there in full force. Sitting round the campfire with camera, mike and 'dolly birds' was a black man whose face was familiar to me from the telly. He said that he and his friend had been to Greenham to do some filming at Christmas time, and they had come back again to do some more. I sat down next to Ann and May, while Margaret talked to this bloke, who told us his name was Kenny Lynch.

It was all rather predictable, but after only a few minutes Sally and Cleis appeared through the trees, looking very determined. They asked Kenny what the film was for, and he and the other man said for the archives. "What archives?" asked Cleis. "My archives", the man with the camera admitted.

They were then asked what right had they to burst into someone's sitting room (which is what our campfire area is) and record us without so much as a by your leave. Cleis said that she remembered that rather the same thing had happened at Christmas time, and she felt they should go. Wow, they were shattered, but after a bit of argument, got up and left us, with comments about belligerent women etc. What was interesting was that even when the two women with them were asked direct questions, they were so male dominated that they hardly answered.

I know damn well that this does not do the 'Greenham image' much good but the intrusion of this sort is done without any understanding of what we are doing.

Another type of tourist we get is the car full of passengers, which drives very slowly past, perhaps stops and takes a photo, then moves on. *Who the hell are these people?* They have come to see the freaks in the zoo, but dare not stop and get involved. To get to our gate, they have to drive off the road and do an actual detour, so there is no excuse of just driving past. If you stand and look them in the eye, they turn away. We are just a spectacle, like a burnt down building that made the news on the telly the night before. They just want to say that they have seen us.

I must say that most or our visitors are lovely. They come to give support, open the boots of their cars and produce food, wood, clothes, blankets, drink and/or money. Most of them wear good warm clothes and footwear when they are sitting round the fire, having a coffee. I am not sure if they are residents from other gates, or just day visitors. The one sure way to tell is to look at their hands. The colour is quite different.

A couple of hours after the Kenny Lynch episode, a mini bus drew up with male and female students from Leicester University: they wanted to film us! They were a bit surprised, but in the end quite agreeable that the women should do all the filming and interviewing. The men could watch, but not could enter into the discussion. They asked permission to take a few still pics, which was fine.

After the interview, which Kay, Anne and I mostly gave (with Bruce Kent turning up in the middle to distribute Mars bars, which he said he thought would he rather different from the usual gifts) the women crew agreed that we were correct in wanting them to keep the men out of the way. They said that they would be back on their own sometime soon.

Nice as all these people were, I needed a bit of fresh air and peace, so went for a walk with Cleis, having done some wood chopping and sorting for relaxation. We went along the fence towards the Yellow Gate, some of the way with a young woman whose father is a Kent County Councillor, very conservative and right wing. His daughter lives in Derbyshire. *I don't think you will ever get her to your political way of thinking, Mr Peter Heath.*

Jill was there when we got back, so we had a talk with her and others. By this time, the visitors were leaving, so it was getting quieter. Kay and Isia were going to come to London with me in the car, so we arranged a 7am start. Our night watch was from Wales, Mag, had come earlier and her two friends came after supper. The Swedish women cooked the meal, and we found the bottle of scotch and wine donated during the day. I felt a great urge to do a little cutting, and Ann said she would come with me. Unfortunately, it was a very quiet, still night, but we did a detour that took us past the shit pits and up to the road past the little cluster of trees. We hid quietly in them for a moment or two until the patrolling soldier was some way off, then I snipped happily for some moments, I almost cut my triangle, before Anne said he was coming back. We retreated into the trees and went back to the campfire. All very satisfying. I do think that I have to keep my hand in, and the fence in disrepair.

There was no sign of M. Sally, Cleis and I felt that we should talk to her, but although we looked quite a few times in the evening, there was no sign of her. Actually, in the end we found out that she had been down to the travelling people and spent some hours with them. When she came back to the camp she talked to the night watch for hours, and seemed quite all right, rather high, but not too bad, then she went off and slept in her car. Jill and I will have to leave any discussion with M to Sally and Cleis after we have gone.

The next morning I got up before six and had some breakfast with Anne and the night watch, before waking Kay and Isia. I left a note in Marion's car as she had gone to bed early the night before. Jill was wandering around, about to go to work, but the others were all asleep. I knew I could not go there again for about three to four weeks. Sally's mother would have come and gone by that time, and perhaps the bailiffs would have flattened the whole of Orange Gate.

I feel an essential part of Greenham, but I am not, or not more than most others. As long as we know why we are there what we are doing, we will come back and be essential for the time we are there, then go again, but always return. But that world goes on without me, however hateful that thought may be.

18th – 19th March 1984

Just two days at Greenham, after a short tour of southern England. First, I stayed with Isobel & Peter and had my interview at Sussex University. Then on to my mother at Worthing, then to Southampton to stay with Di, then on Sunday morning after breakfast, Greenham. Di and I spent some time discussing the Dover project, but for the time being this had been postponed, but will certainly take place sometime in the future. Di was rather worried how to get a message to American Liz at the Blue Gate about a meeting in Winchester that afternoon, so I drove straight there to give her details and money for the meeting. When I got to Blue Gate, I saw Liz and another woman carrying things from the woods towards the other women. I gave them a hand with a large pallet, which was going to be used for *'a portable bender'* with trolley wheels.

I did not stay long, but took a good look at the effect of evictions on all the north gates. It is a very bleak life there now, just the odd bender, rather hastily constructed, and a few tents and the usual piles of cartons with food, wood, etc. in. This weekend we were lucky as the weather was cold but fine and no wind, but this north side is always cold and draughty. I gave a wave to Violet at Indigo, and was pleased to see that there was a car and three or four women. Also at Red, which has no constructions at all, just a fire and women who try to be there as often as possible.

At Orange, there were a dozen or so women, some of whom I had not seen for ages. Ruth, and Jane, and Zoe, and Ruth from Skye, as well as Sally, Jill, Ann Francis, Isia with Lucy, and the newcomers Sue, Ellie, Christine, Liz and others. The usual influx of visitors arrived all day, with food, clothes, wood, etc., etc. We sat and had a meal and caught up on all the news. I heard that E had gone back to her special school, but only after a bit of pressure from the social worker. Margaret was on holiday this weekend, but when Cleis had had a word to her, everything and everyone had become extremely fraught and up tight. The incident is over, but not really forgotten, I am afraid.

I read out loud some of my diary pieces to women round the campfire, and they all seemed to think it was worthwhile carrying on, so I am! Sue, who had not been to Greenham before, as she was afraid that her past life might catch up with her (she had been stabbed seven times, a few years ago), was really over the moon with enthusiasm for more action in the base. Sally, Jill and I agreed to accompany her round and show her as much as possible. We went in my car, first to Yellow where we stopped and talked to Rebecca and others then went on round to Green, where we walked for a while to show Sue the silos, and the fences, which are now amazing. Rows of them. Jill showed us where she had got in some time before, and we all agreed that this is the area that we must all try and get inside, but it really is a frightening sight. Round to the Blue and along that north fence. It really would be quite easy to get in from there, but it is so far from any important part of the base, that it is really not worth it. It is still important to harass and keep snipping, but not to try to get inside for no real reason. Back at Orange, Ruth felt she would like a little snipping party that night. We had two pairs of cutters, mine and one other. Half a dozen of us would go and find a good place. Ruth looked for some more cutters hidden on the common, and we found them, but they were enormous, and very hard to use, so we decided to stick to the usual small ones. We also found a '*baby*' and my orange towrope but decided to leave them there for future use. A couple of the women went off to get some wine, and we had a meal, then we six took off our ponchos, put on dark clothes and headed for the usual corner towards the Yellow Gate. It was a still night but those bloody guard dogs from the wood yard, starting barking, and there were plenty of soldiers around. Ruth and I rather lost the others, but went on round the corner where the Royal Irish Rangers were moaning like hell about discipline, and they were fed up with it. There were too many soldiers around, so we headed back towards our camp. A rather bored soldier was on his own, and we said "good evening" to him. He asked us if we were going to cut the fence, and as far as he was concerned that was fine as he was getting out of the army next Monday. He had paid £100 to get out and had a job as an electrician lined up in Germany. We said we did not want to get him into trouble by cutting on his patch, but he told us to go ahead, that was fine by him, as long as it was not too big. I cut away happily for some minutes, and then Ruth asked him if he would like a drink, and of course, he said yes. We left him standing in front of a nice sized hole in the fence, and went back to my car, got a bottle of scotch and a plastic cup out, and handed him a cup full through the hole. He said cheers and thanks, and we left him. I hope his job and future life are good for him. Next day I had a look at the hole was still there and the cup was outside the hole on the ground, obviously chucked though the hole!

Back at the campfire we had some more to drink and lots of chat etc. After another little walk, I eventually went to bed in Ann from Reading's bender, where I slept soundly until 9 o'clock. By that time, quite a lot of the women had gone, Jill to work, Sue and Liz to London, and we thought we were going to have a quiet day. The first priority was to clear up the campfire area and kitchen bender as it all looked really grotty after a day of visitors, and high living. I tackled the fire area and got rid of a lot of grot, and put the rubbish on the common for the bailiffs to collect, helped a bit in the kitchen then started talking to two women and a man draped with cameras and notebooks. They were of course reporters. One woman from Brazil, the man from Switzerland, and the photographer from England (she apologised for that!) I took them back to the fire, we all had a coffee, and I tried to tell them about Greenham. I know it will come out all wrong, it always does, but I suppose in Brazil, it's just good to know that Greenham news does get there when their own problems such as inflation at 300 per cent per year, existing must be their prime concern.

Isia decided to make us a tortilla, and I wrapped potatoes in foil and put them in the fire. This was for lunch but we did not get round to eating until about 2.30. We just had scones and coffee at about 12.30. Oh the deprived life style of us poor Greenham women. I do not think we should get the Nobel Peace Prize, but we should definitely be in the *Egon Ronay Good Food Guide*. I am not sure whether the hygiene would pass the test, too much grease on the trees round the fire might let us down, but the food and drink are superb, even if we do share the bottle, cup, and plate at times. I do not think germs have much chance with wood smoke and fresh air, apart from Christine the lawyer's terrible cough, which she had brought with her, we are very healthy.

Rebecca came round with a load of packs from a swarm of Swedish women who are going to stay at Orange. On the whole, we are always pleased to have women, but we all feel that it is far better if these groups break up rather more, two or three at each gate, rather than all at one. Anyway we will suggest this to them when they appear. Soon after this, Rose arrived in a panic. It was 4.30 but evictions were starting on the north side. We leapt into the only two cars we had, plus some wood, polythene and things to sleep on, plus a large water container. First to Indigo, where the women were sitting round a fire, but seemed to be OK if rather subdued. We left

Ruth there, and went on to Violet. Here Liz and Annie showed me the mobile bender, which was full of gear, so we went on to Blue. The Council dustcart, bailiffs, police, dustmen etc., and my most unfavourite local resident were all there in force. I wanted to spit in her eye, but everyone sad that she was not worth doing time for, and they were right. There were sad piles of possessions everywhere. I opened the back of my car, and told women to pile everything in that they could, and I would take it round to Green for safekeeping. I ended up, not being able to see out of the back mirror, but had the first aid carton, a tent, polythene, food, odds and sods, and took these off to green with a Blue Gate woman. We put the things by the side of the road, and then I went back again to help some more. At one point, I found myself with a couple of women pulling a large sheet of polythene away from a bailiff, and when we won, stuffing it in my car. Then I helped to carry the kitchen table up the path into the woods, where we hid it behind a gorse bush. Back by the gate, Annie was singing a protest song, and we all joined in the chorus. The last of the items was shoved into a van. We stood around, until eventually, the police, bailiffs and dustcart drove off. The dustcart is one of the crusher sort, so anything that goes in will not come out again. It is all very final. Anyway, there was nothing more I could do, so I gave the women the rest of the stuff still in my car, and went back to the other gates to pick up my passengers. At Violet, I asked if there was anything I could do to help, as there were nine women there with nothing apart from a fire. They asked for fish and chips, so American Liz and another woman came with me back to Orange where I dropped Isia off, and picked up two Swedish women who were going to Violet for the night. It was quite dark of course by this time, but on the road to Thatcham. I recognised a figure with a backpack. I jumped on my brakes, yelled "Miranda", terrified my passengers, and leapt out of the car. Miranda was looking her usual controlled self. She was glad when I offered to take her gear, even though I had no room for her. She went on to Orange, and the rest of us went to Thatcham. The chip shop order was for: "12 chips, 9 fish & chips and 4 large chips". Nobody turned a hair.

I dropped my women off at the various gates and went home to Orange. Supper seems to have come and gone, but I handed round the bottle of red wine I had bought, plus the chips. I am not sure quite where the bottles of scotch and rum appeared from, but I was very careful that night, as really there are certain things I could not remember about the previous night, particularly as to the whereabouts of my bolt cutters. Actually careful Jill had them put in her bender, and I was pleased to get them back. They have been with me for a long time, and have cut much fence. I should hate to lose them.

I was not sure which bender I was going to sleep in. Ann from Reading was there, so I moved my stuff from the bender. Sally thought I should sleep in Miranda's, but it was so perfect, virginal, white, with flowers in a jam jar, that I didn't feel I could intrude. Jill, Ruth and Margaret from Violet Gate all wanted to stay at Red in Gore-Tex survival bags, as we were all convinced that the Cruise convoy would come out that night. There were masses of extra police being drafted into the base, and all day there had been an exercise inside, with American voices and vehicles tearing about, and yelling over loudspeakers that this is 'a yellow alert'. These exercises make my blood run cold. Apart from anything else, the vehicles inside all have fixed mortar type guns mounted on them, and I know that most of the soldiers would not question a command to point these at us women, and fire. During my constant driving round the base, I could see vehicles parked in odd places in the base. Anyway, Jill said I could have her bender, and Ellie joined me. It was a rather short night, as by 5 o'clock I was awake, and got up soon after as I wanted to leave by six, as I had to go to work in Dover by 9am. I had a coffee, collected Isia and Lucy, said goodbye to Barbara the night watch, Anne who had done an early stint, Sally, who had just got up very early, and Ellie, whom I had thoroughly wakened.

Isia and I drove along the north fence, checked that Jill, Ruth and Margaret were OK. Jill was awake and glad to see us. Then we just saw the other gates with women outside, lying by fires, trying to sleep. We gave them a wave, and I have decided that I will be back on 29th March with the Peace Van, as this will be very helpful with the evictions.

The song of the week at Greenham starts like this:

> *The raindrops are falling on my head,*
> *The bailiffs have crushed my bender*
> *And taken away my bed ....*

29th March – 6th April 1984

I have never tried to do this before, actually writing about Greenham from there, sitting in the car on the morning after, in my poncho and mittens. I had better start with yesterday; as that is the day it all happened.

I heard on the radio that the cruise convoy had been taken out again, and realised that it was from Blue Gate that it had happened, as the familiar routine of pinning the women to the fence was very predictable. Of course, I felt that I would not have stayed in London, but I know damn well that my presence at Blue or any other Gate would have made no difference at all. It was a slow drive until I got to the M4 as it was *Stop-the-City* day and there were masses of cars around. All was fine until I turned the corner of Orange Gate, and then to my horror I realised that all the benders had gone. Nothing. Just the fence and rather chewed up ground. I couldn't believe it. It was all so desolate. However, the campfire was there and so were the Orange Gate Women. Sian, Ann, Ann and Jill (these three turned up a bit later as they were in court), Maureen, Christine, Sally, Rebekah, Miranda, Anne with the hair, Julie who is new, and Jane and Liz who arrived much later. We sat for a while and had a coffee, but I was feeling restless and we heard that evictions were going on, including Green Gate so Christine and I went to see what was happening. All the north road gates were looking very empty indeed, just a few women at each, with a small fire, and practically no possessions, just odd bits of food and plastic bags. We stopped and talked to some, and although they were feeling very low at the thought of the cruise convoy coming out just a few hours before there was no way that they were going to be moved from their gates. It appears that the police had been very rough in their handling of the women and it had been quite unnecessary, so they were upset by this, as much as the bringing out the convoy.

By the time we got round to Green Gate, the munchers had done their work and there was practically nothing there except a group of women talking to TVS (Television South?) and a muncher waiting to get past them as they stood in the road. The interview was given accompanied by the roar of lorry engine, and when eventually the lorry went off, Christine and I decided to go to Yellow to see what was happening there.

There are always many women there, and it was no exception today. Just after we got there the usual traffic was driving in and out including a couple of big army lorries. Then a small convoy of three more started driving out, someone said it was part of a NATO exercise, and quite spontaneously half a dozen women stood in front of the first vehicle and stopped it. Then more women joined them, and these three vehicles just waited there with engines revving. The driver wound up his window so he could not talk to us. A woman came upon with a can of spray paint and carefully made two feminist symbols on the front of the vehicle, when the police were not looking. I went and had a look at the trailer and pulled the cover off and looked at the equipment in it. I think it was communication electronic stuff. The police told the driver to switch off his engine, so we got our beer and sandwiches out, and prepared for a long blockade. By this time, the TV cameras and other media people were about, and all the normal traffic that uses this main gate constantly, had to be turned back down the road to use other gates. After nearly an hour the order was for the lorries to go back inside the gate, so we watched, with a lot of laughter, the trailer being unhitched and pushed back by the police. Then the most inept piece of driving I've seen for a long time by a soldier, whose glasses completely steamed up in his frustration as he tried to back his big lorry, with the 'help' of women shouting "left hand down, no right hand down" and even the police were roaring with laughter. I helped push the front lorry back and held on to the radiator grill, hoping that I could go inside with it, but the police had other ideas and pulled me off. They had also previously taken a woman in, but released her so as the gate was still shut, she climbed *over* the gate. Eventually they were back inside, and within minutes there appeared right across the entrance an old ambulance belonging to the women, which they parked sideways on to the gate, and let the tyres down. Two women climbed onto the roof, and a mattress and various loads of rubbish were taken from it and piled against the gate. The electric gate (inside the ordinary one) had been buggered by women throwing little pebbles into the grooved track. Outside more and more rubbish was piling up hard against the gate. I went to get my bolt cutters as we thought a little action might be useful, but ended up helping a woman heave the largest 'yuletide' log you have ever seen. By now, a bonfire had been started between the gate and the ambulance, and we put the log on to get a really good-sized fire going.

The police were completely stuck. They had two or three officers trying to control the traffic in the road, and the rest were trapped inside the base. We blockaded the gate completely successfully for some hours with no planning or any idea what we might want to, or be able to, do such a thing. That's Greenham for you. Christine and I felt we ought to come home to Orange, as we were hungry and thought there might be another eviction. We felt that we should be around to help, particularly as the car was essential to pile possessions into.

We had only been back a short while, when the bailiffs, muncher and muncher men arrived. They were in a ruthless mood, and although we tried to direct them to the rubbish and other non-essentials, they crushed a lot of things. I piled everything I could first inside the car, then on top of it. No one tried to touch these things, but we had to argue like mad that the food and water were picnic material, and women sat firmly on water containers and food bins, claiming them. It can't have been nearly so bad as the benders all going four days before, but we all hated seeing stuff just disappear and being chewed up. I rescued a chair which I pulled from one man's hand, and swore it was my personal property as well as various other items, and my passing shot was to pull a wooden spoon tied to a piece of wood from our of the back of the muncher. Not an item of any vital importance I admit, but everything needs rescuing from bailiffs. Jill had insisted on reading the actual piece of paper that authorised the eviction to take place, and has now come up with the idea that we can claim for any personal possessions destroyed by the muncher. In fact, later that afternoon they went into Newbury and saw someone in the legal department of the council who was more than slightly startled when Jill informed him that she had talked to her barrister who said that she must claim for her possessions. Jill was first asked her name and address, which she gave as Lovejoy Peace and her address as the Orange Gate, Greenham Common. When the legal bloke objected, Jill told him that the Greenham address had been accepted by the magistrates, so he shut up. He then asked her what she was claiming for and when she told him one sleeping bag and ten blankets, he turned pale. If all the women made claims like this it could upset the authorities greatly, and would be very interesting.

After the bailiffs left I brought out my bottle of wine, as not only was the sun over the *yardarm*, but we were all feeling rather shattered, sad, furious, upset, but not defeated or downhearted for more than a short while. We cleared up and got ourselves sorted out and decided that Indian take-away would be nice for supper that night. Ann and I ended up with an enormous and complicated list for curries for 12. We made our phone calls in there and had a good wash in boiling hot water, and had a glass of beer each, so our time was not wasted. Back at the camp the food and drink were passed around, but none of us wanted a late night for various reasons (mainly cruise!), and the women were tired. I did offer to stay up for the night watch, but luckily three women from Wales came, and then three more so I left them to fight out who was going to stay here and who was going to another gate, and I got my hottie and crawled into my two sleeping bags in the car.

I had no idea it was going to be such a cold night, but I slept soundly and when Jill and Anne woke me at 6.45 I was amazed to find the frost was as thick inside the car as outside. The night watch had already left, so there was no one near the campfire, and I got up and stayed there, tidied up and got some breakfast.

So, the start of another day. The days go by, and now it is Monday the 2nd April, the day they told us that no women would be left at Greenham Common. Well I am still here and so are many of my friends, although some of us are a little physically battered having just done a partial blockade of Orange Gate. There were not enough of is to be really successful, but at least we held up the flow of traffic for a while. My poncho is torn and my shoulder and arm rather sore, but nothing worse than that. A quiet sit in the car with Kes looking at me, away from women and police, seems necessary for a while, as it is only 8.30. So far, I have had coffee in bed (brought by Sue), coffee and toast at the campfire, done a blockade at the gate, then coffee and hard-boiled egg and toast and honey and now typewriter. It is going to be a long day.

Friday was a quiet day, in fact, I cannot remember a thing that happened, except that the weather was awful and it rained on and off all day. We cleared up the campsite, cooked, communicated, went for a walk along the fence, greeted visitors and women who came to stay, and coped with eight Danish women who turned up. It seems to take a long time to do even a quite simple thing, when the rain and wind are lashing down, and the cover over the fire is falling sideways, so it has to be propped up with a long piece of wood. Then, that falls down on Maureen, so we stick it in the fire grid, and that works, until the wind blows it sideways again and you have to start all over again. It is not easy to live here, but the humour and companionship make it all worthwhile. One problem now is that as there are no benders, there is nowhere to retreat to. Survival bags are all very well, but apart from not being very easy to get in and out of, you can only lie down. When you are in, with the rain beating on it and you, it is not very pleasant. Sally has just come to sit in the car (it is getting crowded as now it has Sue, Kes, Sally, me and camping equipment for about 20 women) and she cannot remember a thing about Friday either.

It is now Tuesday 7.30am. We have just done another blockade, and once again, it is nice to retreat into the car and quiet, especially as I cannot see out, or be seen, as the frost is so thick on the windows.

Saturday and the visitors started to arrive as well as regulars. Sue, and Zoe and Cleis, etc., etc., plus dozens of other women, some whom I recognised and some I didn't. We all felt there would not be any evictions with that number of women around, so we could relax. One sad thing that happened was that the secret bender on the common had been discovered. Sue was getting out of it when a man came along and took a photo of her and said that he was a councillor and that "she was not allowed to camp on the common and must go"

Later that day we took all the hidden goods out of the bender and put them in my car, and then we carried the bender in one piece back near the fire where it has been used ever since. Christine went back home and I did some shopping and tour of the gates.

I have been made Orange Gate money woman, while I am here, as I have a car to keep cash in. I took Julie with me to Thatcham for food and still the wind blew and women (too many of them) tried to huddle round one fire. The Danish women have built themselves a bender in the woods, but they join us for meals, and the whole place gets very crowded. Ellie arrived about teatime the evening became fairly hectic and noisy. Some of the residents gave up the unequal struggle and retired to the portable bender in peace and quiet. I drove the car well away from the noise and Ellie and I had an undisturbed night, with Jill and Sue in their car a bit up the road. At one time, I thought there was snow on the windscreen, but decided that it was just my imagination. Unfortunately, it was not. We had snow flurries and icy northeast winds all day. The women in the Gore-Tex and survival bags are having a tough time. One morning I went quietly into the rabbit warren where they are, and the only thing to be seen are a dozen or so bright orange bags filled with something lumpy. The lumpy object is a woman, plus clothes, sleeping bag, boots, rucksack, in fact all her worldly possessions. There is no sign of hair or head, and the only sure way of finding out which end the head is, is the fact that the frost is melted and the bag is its proper bright orange colour, not coated with white.

On Saturday afternoon, Sue and I gave a long interview for a German woman who is a free-lance journalist. She asked the usual questions about Greenham, and we answered to the best of our ability why we were here etc., and then tried to persuade her to come herself, then she would know more about it. She said that she did not like camping, and we had some difficulty in persuading her that we didn't either, but this had not stopped our coming or involvement with Greenham. I am certain that it will be the same old type of article that she produces in the end, just like everyone else's. I must say that the longer I stay here, the less in some ways I seem to do, and the more I talk in agreement and harmony. We all do I think.

At the moment the sun is shining and it is now beautiful. The frost is melting on the window, so I can see more and more. It is very quiet here. I do not know about round the rest of the base, perhaps they are evicting Yellow at the moment. Quite soon, I must have a really good wash. Personal hygiene is important, especially after nearly a week!

I do not know where all the women came form on Sunday, but they turned up all day, and stayed and made benders on the places where the benders had been evicted. There were picnics, women from other gates turned up and the whole day was a sort of a party. All right. I must admit it. The residents felt pushed out from their own fire and found they could not even get a coffee. The litter that was left was horrible, particularly as we felt that the women who come on these demos should be much more careful and ecology minded. It sounds foul to bitch like this when it is all support, but I am afraid to varying degrees we did get a bit resentful. I helped Ann to build a bender and we encouraged other women standing around to do the same thing. Afterwards we felt that too much wood had been cut and the trees would not recover, and we were certain that in no time at all they would be 'munched'. The odd thing is that they are still there, and women have spent the past couple of nights in them right under the soldier's noses. The previous night young Julie had taken her survival bag over near the fence, and she had been chucked off again and again by the MoD police, but when there are a lot of us around, they are not quite so keen and macho.

Ellie, Julie and many others went home that evening, and later I went and phoned John, my mother and Mark. When I came back, I got the car sorted out for Lynne to move in with me for the night, as the rabbit warren was pretty full. Sue said she would wake us in the morning with tea and coffee at 6.45. We had a quiet evening; I think we were all tired after the activity and movement of so many people during the day. There is nowhere to retreat to without benders, but this is till home, for women and we want quiet and space, time to think, read, write, and perhaps communicate just on a one to one basis. I am particularly aware of this 'space' need this time, and I do have a car I can shut myself in. Home at Greenham is something very special and it can be destroyed by the invasion of privacy and tactlessness of women who are insensitive to the fact that just a fire and no real structure can mean security, love and perhaps be the most important place in the world to some women. It is not easy for an outsider to see a lump of fence and rather muddy ground and a few broken down old chairs, and a palette, which is called a coffee table, to mean so much, and actually to be living room.

Sue brought us our early morning tea and coffee and about 20 of us tried a blockade. We were too far from the gate, and it was not much of a success, but we did hold things up for a while. We shoved masses of things in my car in case the bailiffs came. After a while, we heard that nothing was happening anywhere very much, so decided to go round to the other gates, as we had promised Jill to remind them to tell everyone, word of mouth only about painting the fence on 7th May. Sue, Lynne and I set off, but the back of the car was so piled up with stuff that I backed into a visitor's car and broke the rear cover on my brake light. We did the round and there were dozens of women sitting around, and at Yellow, the media were very much in evidence. Anyway, nothing happened, it was all quiet and peaceful, and so we came home again. I sat in the car and talked to Sue for ages, then to Rebekah. When Ruth and Penny came, then Moira and Jan from Tunbridge Wells, I knew it was going to be an evening of good singing, not the usual tuneless stuff. Then Rebecca from Yellow came, and I was glad Jane and I had done a quick wine run, as the ballads and songs were really good.

We went to bed quite early, but I should mention that at 5pm all the gates were doing another blockade. I do not think ours was the best. We always seem to have about an equal number of women versus police, and without doubt, they are bigger, stronger and definitely more brutal than we are. We had another blockade this morning. That is three in two days, and enough for me. Let my bruises fade before I do anymore.

Maureen has told me she will put on a kettle for coffee and a large container for washing. It sounds too good to be true!

4th April 1984

Well I had a fantastic bath, starting with hair, then body, feet, and then clothes all in the same water, with hottie water for rinsing. I really felt clean after that. The only slight annoyance was the plane with the trailer reading 'Ratepayers say good riddance, girls' but I was not put off, just stood there naked and waved to the pilot. It was a beautiful day after the early frost. Hot sunshine, and in the afternoon after I had been to Thatcham for shopping, and to try to get the part for my car. After that, we sat in the warren and sunbathed. Actually, the car part was quite funny, as the garage did not have it in stock, so they promised to have it for me by this morning. The store man was extremely polite, called me madam, and asked for my name. I then waited for him to ask my address, and if he had and I answered Orange Gate, Greenham Common, I have an awful feeling that his tone might have altered.

We relaxed in the rabbit warren. It felt good to do nothing and just sit and talk and play the fool generally. All this took place with silly French accents, but it is a good way to unwind, and wait for the next event. Jane actually wore shorts, and I got down to tee shirt and removed leg warmers. Unfortunately, this sort of existence does not go on forever, and at about 4.30 we were aware of a lot of MoD cops in vans all around the place. Suddenly they moved in and started removing women and the benders over by the fence. We all went over to support the women there and sat down by the fire. We were asked to move, and when we refused, they carried and dragged us across the road. I actually got carried in style on the chair I was sitting on, but they were getting rather heavy and unpleasant, so we had to be a bit careful. I did a head count. As there were at least 30 police, they far outnumbered us. Then they pulled the benders down and dragged them to the base gate, so we pulled all our rubbish over the road for them to take inside as well. The police did not like this and hurled the bags back across the road to us, and tempers were staring to flare. They told us that we must not go on MoD property, even just to walk on it was trespass. In the end, we gave up, and they went home, so we had supper. The Danish women were still here; they were going very early the next day and said they would do a night watch for us.

I had bought a bottle of wine, but there were so many women round the fire, it would have meant about one sip each. So on the way to get something from the car I passed Rebekah asked her to have a drink, then Ann from Reading arrived, then Sally, Miranda, Lynne, Jane, and in the end when we were drunk and stoned. We felt we should not leave Anne and vicar's wife out, so I was delegated to fetch her tactfully. By the time she was also in the car, there were eight of us. We decided (very drunkenly) that we ought to cut a hole in the fence bug enough to drive the car in, turn sharp right and then out through the base gate! Well it was novel idea and very funny indeed at the time, although the soldiers did not think so. They all got quite worried, and we were making enough noise to waken the dead. Maureen then arrived with the idea that if I drove the car fast at the fence with Sally on top, then stopped-hard, she would perhaps fly over, or through, the fence. Eventually we decided it was time for bed, and filled hotties and went our separate ways. The trouble was that I had had some unbelievably strong coffee and didn't get to sleep for a while. At 2.30am, Astrid knocked politely on the car window, woke me, and told me that the bailiffs would definitely be here at 4am.

I am not sure where she got her information from but when she suggested waking the others to tell them, I advised her not to. Nor, to rouse them at 3.30. When the bailiffs arrived, there would be time enough. I got to sleep again, and the next thing I knew was Astrid once more knocking politely at the car window to say goodbye to me. She is a nice woman. Yesterday, I had done an audio recording for her. Afterwards, I had suggested that in future I am sure the Danish women would gain much more, and so would we, if they split themselves into smaller groups of only two or three per gate. We did find them a little overpowering, but they are marvellous to come to Greenham at all. I think we must be sure to communicate on a more personal basis, rather than a huge unwieldy bunch, with language problems to boot. Women who come to Greenham should always come in ones and twos, otherwise they are a group, not individuals, and as Miranda describes it, it is hard to make eye contact.

Well today is not so quiet. The eviction of Yellow took place in the early hours of the morning. We sorted out the rabbit warren, piled our stuff into my car and waited. One problem was that Margaret's car would not start, so I drove her and Ann to Thatcham to get a train for Reading and the Crown Court. They have to go every day for a fortnight. They come back each night very tired and drained.

Who knows how the rest of the day will be. We will get food, talk, exist, and wait for our eviction. Yellow Gate women are right, it is almost a relief when it comes, but while it is actually happening, it is degrading and unbelievably horrible. My car is full of my friends' personal possessions, and we have many visitors already this morning. We shall just have to wait and see.

5th April 1984

Well it happened, but we were quite ready for the eviction. By the time it came in the afternoon, we had a mass of visitors with cars as well as Marion's and mine; she turned up just in time! The Orange Gate was in an awful mess and we carefully left a lot of rubbish around in bags in secret places so that the bailiff's men could take them. It worked a treat. They leapt into the gorse with the police and really had a good search. They did, unfortunately, find the other hidden bender, which was a shame, and they tried to take away Miranda's little half bender which she uses to cover her Gore-Tex and survival bag. She had painted on it in large clear letters **"Miranda's Personal Property"**. Although they tried to evict it, we shouted at them and they left it. They managed to run over it, but did not do a lot of damage. My car was packed with items as usual, including the cover for the fire, which was tied, not very securely on the roof. All the cars were full of food, bins, wood, personal goods, water containers, polythene, the tools, chairs, etc., etc. Everything important. We did leave in a very prominent place the Charles & Diana mug, which was taken, luckily. Also a tin opener that did not open tins.

The police were being quite heavy. They thought they had us by the short and curlies as we were informed that we could not park our cars on the Common as the bailiffs would have us, and if we parked on the road, the police would have us. So we drove off. I had a notice sticking out of my back window, saying "Business as Usual" and "We're still Here", and the polythene flapping around. We went round to Violet, and found three women sitting round a fire with nothing there, but after a few minutes, other women came back from the bushes carrying water and food. Someone had hurled a tin full of herbal teabags and some mugs in my car just as I was driving off, so, they found me some coffee and handed over the tea. We did discuss parking the cars that night in a big lay-by near Violet, but in the end, it was not necessary. I came back to Orange and found the police were still wandering around. There was a slight panic as Sian had been caught. She was under some sort of warrant for non-payment of fine, so Rebekah took £100 from the moneybox and went to find her, and I removed the sheeting from the car and decided to do the grand tour.

On my way to Yellow, I was stopped. I think the notice sticking out of the car window may have alerted the police to me. They asked to see my driving licence and insurance papers. Of course, the insurance stuff is back home, so I have to go to the local cop shop on Monday in Deal. At Yellow, the women were all sitting on the ground opposite their normal area. There is now a wooden fence surrounding the area with police every few yards guarding it. Already women had set up a kitchen area, and were sorting out their food. Others just sat around talking and gaining strength, before starting to live again in their normal style. There were many women there. They were strong, and were certainly not going to be moved.

At Green it was as if nothing had happened, except that they had not lit their fire again. All their goods had been stashed in the sanctuary; so they just had to put everything back again when they felt the time was right.

At Blue, the women were just sitting around on the muddy ground, assuring me and everyone that they were so used to being evicted and having a hard time, that this was no different and of course they would survive, and if they weren't allowed fires, they were strong, and would just be a bit cold for a while. Violet still had the mobile bender and their furniture was just being returned to them from a van. I knew Lizzie, Annie, Judy and co would survive with much humour and happiness. It is another gate like ours with this awful French accent, which we cannot stop doing. It becomes very exhausting, especially when I looked at my watch early this morning and said to myself in an awful pseudo accent "*Ah yees, eet iss nearly zeven.*" We do manage to laugh a lot with it though. I have a feeling that this is what has made me lose my voice today. I am being really quite silent by my standards.

I got back to Orange the same time as Marion and found that our fire had been relighted and the possessions put back in place. Marion had brought food with her, so we did not even have to cook. We just heat everything up. It was magnificent. I passed the bottle of scotch round as we were all rather exhausted, if not downhearted, and so the evening started. The night watch turned up, some fairly local visitors to find out if we had survived and to see how we were managing. Visitors, including Liz and Hannah came, and went, and although we all felt that cruise might come out that night we were too tired to both much. Maureen felt she ought to stay up for a while with the night watch, but as the fire was so nice, I do not think it was much of a hardship.

It was an icy night, but the frost cleared quite quickly in the sunshine. Another beautiful day. I decided that after breakfast I would have a bath and wash my hair in the bowl. Overall, it has been a pretty quiet day. The police came round here twice this morning with an old-fashioned galvanised watering can, and piddled with it on the fire to put it out. There is this stupid by-law about no fires on the common, so just to harass us, they put out fire out and we light it again when they are not looking or have gone away.

It is now the next day, Friday I think and it has been all go, since I was so rudely interrupted yesterday. Liz and Hannah from Indigo came for a visit and said they wanted action. A huge transporter plane came in during the afternoon (just before Bruce Kent arrived with the Mars bars and a bottle of scotch, *we were honoured!*). Liz watched carefully and saw that what was taken from the plane was not put into the silo, but in one of the large hangers that is almost equidistant from Orange and Violet Gates. Liz and Hannah felt it was worth going inside to find out what it was, and we discussed the possibility of two or three actions taking place at the same time. Jane, MohicAnne and I joined them on an extraordinary cross-country expedition in the area of the golf club. Most of the time we seemed to be completely in the wrong direction, away from the fence, crashing through undergrowth fording muddy streams, etc., etc. It was all quite fun but not really very helpful. We walked miles, and in the end got back to Violet and then Indigo and then I drove MohicAnne back to Orange when it was quite dark and there were hundreds of women around, all eating fantastic food. By this time, the vegetarian diet was having some effect on me, and all I wanted was good solidifying scrambled eggs. I had them with garlic bread and flapjacks, wine, scotch etc., and they did me the power of good.

We then discussed the action in some detail and decided that there was absolutely no reason for us to do our action with Indigo, but if we did it vaguely at the same time, it might be a good idea. We then discussed numbers. Seven of us were prepared, and so we donned dark clothes and set off. I am afraid I was being a bit Brown Owlish and suggested that we went through the common, down the road and then climbed up the hill through the trees. This was fine but the bracken and brambles made it hard going. MohicAnne had the other cutters and we went ahead. There was a lovely piece of fence with only one spotlight shining on me and so I sat down and started snipping. It was a very still and quiet night and the noise of each snip sounded like gunfire to me. The soldiers could hear me but could not locate my position, and torches were flashing like mad all over the place. In the end I cut a hole low down, large enough to crawl through, so I stuck my feet inside and started cutting the barbed wire. Then there was a shout. I had been spotted, so I got out and we all tore down the hill and then waited quietly before going home along the road, in an exaggeratedly drunken fashion. When we turned up our road, there were police and cars around, and Maureen and I decided that it would be a good idea to hide the cutters for a while by a tree (we retrieved them later.) Back at the fire, we had another drink or two and Christine arranged that she would sleep in my car, but would come to bed later on. It was a bit of a squash, as I had two or three rucksacks as well as other things. We did manage and Ruth brought me coffee in bed in the morning. Incidentally, we found out that we had been much more successful than Liz and co. They had not even got to the fence, much less started to cut it. I think they were quite impressed with our effort.

Today. Well, eviction this morning, but we were pretty well prepared for it, although that does not make it any better. We put all out food etc. in the van, which does not start, and masses of other things in my car and everywhere. I do not think they got that much stuff. It is just the hassle, and tiredness that it produces. I went round with my load to Violet, and then came back here again. So far, during the rest of the day (it's now 6pm), the police have been round with their piddling little fire extinguishers and put out our fire for the 5th or 6th time. It is pathetic, it really is. I shall never have respect for police again after the way I have seen them behave at Greenham this week.

Back home again now, with Gus (the cat) sitting next to me. Those ten days are very important in my life. They reaffirm the importance of the place, or to be more accurate, the women who are there. It is the trust and unity of is, against them, the 'them' being authority, particularly when represented by men in uniform. Oddly enough, the incident that made me the most furious was when I was stopped in my car, when driving round with a load of stuff after one eviction. This was an enormous invasion of privacy. I am a law-abiding citizen on the road, my car is in excellent repair, and I bitterly resent that I can be pulled into the side by cops and asked for my credentials. They were polite, fine, but it is the principal I am against. When I took my insurance note into Deal police station on Sunday afternoon, the officer made a note of everything, and when he had finished he asked me if I'd had a bump in the car in Berkshire, and I firmly told him I hadn't, but I'd been stopped because I was a Greenham Woman.

10th April 1984

At home, I realise how tired I am, mentally rather than physically. It is an effort to do all the cooking, washing up, living, etc. at ground level. My knees get a bit stiff, particularly with sitting on the ground or a log. Also, crawling through bracken and brambles and gorse can be quite tiring. Even sleeping for nights on end in the car, although it is fairly comfortable, isn't exactly luxury. Although without doubt, I sleep longer and sounder there than I do at home, although I do wake a bit stiff. Actually, now at home I have been opening the window over my head wide, and it does work. I am not sure it is not due to the breathing of cold air; which does the trick for me. Back here one of my problems is to do and think things that are not connected with Greenham. I live and love it, but I do have another life back here and University soon, which I must prepare for in many ways. It is no help having Mother in hospital and a trip to Worthing for the day yesterday is really not what I wanted. Poor old girl. When I first saw her, she looked so old, vulnerable and lost. I just hope that my end will be with a bang not a whimper, but how long does one go on? I keep thinking of the time I have wasted, but I suppose we all think this. One of the ways that Greenham has helped me is that Deal is now no longer the only place where I have friends. I can pick up the phone and call many women and I am certain that I would be made welcome for a few days anyway. This is chance to get away, and it will happen more and more. This weekend I have to be the Greenham woman *talker* at the demo in Dover. The following I am going to Liverpool to see Mark, then the next two weekends at Greenham again. Ouch! I haven't told John this yet.

27th – 28th April 1984

This is the shortest time I have stayed at Orange, but with my mother being in hospital I felt I had to come here (Worthing) after only 24 hours. I rather stole the time at Greenham anyway, to gain strength, meet up with everyone. Also, it must be admitted, have a good time. Well, all those things happened and now I am in the totally artificial world of Worthing, my Mother's flat, and the knowledge that I am no further forward with anything much. I was prepared to tackle doctors, surgeons, the entire National Health Service, but never thought that no-one important had made any decision on whether to operate or not. About the only thing I have achieved is a decent suntan from being outdoors for those 24 hours of fantastic hot sunshine.

I drove up to Greenham via Guildford, and I am not sure that this was the right route. It took over two hours and I got here soon after 1pm. I was told at the campfire that there was a general/money meeting in the rabbit meadow, so set off there. Jill, Sally, Ruth, Penny, Rebekah, Anne from Reading, Isia and a Turkish friend and her young son, Miranda, Jan the waffle woman, Jo and Maria who now live here rather than Yellow, Mira who is on the world cycle tour, etc., etc. and of course the night watch, all were there or turned up during the time I was there. There were more than 40 women from other gates at the money meeting, and a great deal was thrashed out, although there was no real conclusion to anything. It was an interesting meeting in many ways, as personal grievances were aired over personalities, some women were in tears at times, but I think everyone had a chance to have a say of some sort. One of the real problems over money is how it should be administered. We do get many donations and in the building society, there is something like £9,000. At the moment little money is coming in, and a lot of money is going out. There are obviously various outgoings for food, dole money, general expenses, but how these requests should be funded each week is a problem. Some women feel that too much money goes to individuals for what could be seen as rather frivolous requests. Everyone felt that Yellow had more than its fair share of money, but on the other hand, small gates like Violet, Indigo and Turquoise, did not need much.

I really was aware that there was a lot of *gateism* at a meeting like this, as different types of women do gravitate to different gates. One suggestion was that the seven gates should have an equal amount of money each week to sort out as the women, but others said this would not be fair, as some had more visitors as well as regulars to cope with. One woman said that there women from other gates didn't visit, and therefore when requests were made at the weekly money meetings, women from other gates had no idea of the integrity of the woman asking for money. If someone needed money for a holiday, it might be essential for that particular woman to have it, but not for another. Trust had to be maintained by women there otherwise we could not exist.

There was another long discussion as to whether we had any use at all in being at Greenham. Had we outlived our usefulness? Cruise missiles were in the base, and the convoys had come out, and in fact had just brushed us aside. Most of us felt that it was vital that we were there, and the image of Greenham gave strength to the entire peace movement throughout the world, as well as small women's groups and local CND. If there were no Peace Camps at Greenham, this would be a terrible failure on our part for peace, but also as supportive women we would have nowhere to go and there would be no completely free centre for women to live and express themselves as we can do here. Most of us agreed that we had come to Greenham from CND or peace groups in the first place. Nevertheless, once we were here, other issues took hold, and however frustrated and even bitter we felt at times, we would stay.

The only really positive thing that we all agreed was that the meeting had aired many issues, which were important, vital to us. There was a suggestion that the money being divided into seven equal parts could be put into practice for a trial period to see how it worked out, and those with surplus cash could donate excess to causes they felt useful. For this week, things would go on as usual and another meeting was arranged for next week to sort out this new scheme.

Wow, this was not exactly an easy meeting, but I was glad to have been present. My only contribution was that there was no way that Greenham women should think of leaving. Although we still needed more women to come and stay to give the regulars a break, and more chance of holidays away from the tensions of life there.

We staggered back to the campfire and put on sweaters, as it was getting cool by this time. I decided that it was high time I slept out in the rabbit meadow, borrowed a Gore-Tex and put my sleeping bags in it. I had brought some mushrooms, someone else some frozen peas, plus rice and some pasta, and Miranda produced a meal, and the drink was brought out. Ann cut my hair and the evening started. Io produced her clarinet and another woman a duck decoy whistle, and the songs and music started. We went over to the gate, and I stood on my head, just for fun! Back to fire and party games, and then as I was tired I left a lot of them and went to my sleeping bag with hottie and cup of water. It really was a lovely night, and the stars were bright. A nightingale sang for hours (near the shit pit I think). I took a long time to get to sleep, but I did not mind, as I was warm and fairly comfortable, although my hips rather stuck in the ground. I was surprised at some time during the night when taking a sip of water to find that it had a thick layer of ice on it, and I certainly did find the air very cold to breathe at times. The dawn chorus took over eventually, and I slept and dozed until about 9am.

Breakfast at the campfire was nice, but it was much colder in that draughty spot than in the rabbit meadow, so before long I put on my shorts and went back there. Most of the regulars drifted in and it was so hot that before long most of us were in varying degrees of undress. It was marvellous. I read my book for a while, talked, Isia's very good essay on photography was read to us by Sally, and then Miranda and Jan read my last piece on Greenham out. If ever I do get this writing together, Penni will illustrate it.

There were no evictions or police putting out the fire, apart from one at about midnight, although this happens all the time on weekdays. There is little round the fire, and the women from other gates were amazed that we still had any chairs left at all. Food and wood were in short supply this weekend, and I hope that more came after I left, as they were badly needed. We shared a lunch of rice and tuna salad and at about 3pm I got ready to go. I pinned up the broken zip on my trousers, which I had broken while standing on my head, and said goodbyes. All being well I shall be back in less than a week. Next Friday, I hope.

4th – 7th May 1984

I got to Greenham exactly a week ago, but it feels like a lifetime. Since I left there, I've had a day's work, played golf (very badly) been at home, organised mother-in-law and Aunt Marjorie, and have come back to Worthing again, collected my mother from hospital and now she is resting, and I am typing.

This time I went to Orange Gate via Worthing and a visit to my mother in hospital with Hilary, who has not been to Greenham since before Christmas. Mind you, she knows as much about the place as I do, as for months I have been telling her about it, the women, the life, the evictions, the actions, etc. I was relieved to find that it had not suddenly all changed, as she might have thought I was just a liar!

It was a marvellous weekend, culminating in the painting of Orange gate, orange, a bit pinkish perhaps, but the overall effect is great. There are so many women I knew there, from the regulars, Miranda, Sally and Anne, Jill, Ruth and Penni, Rebekah and Cathy, Charlie, Sian, Jay, Isia & Ellen, Liz from Cornwall, Margaret, Io & Maria, Lynne and Welsh friends, Maureen, Cleis etc. Then the more casuals, Christine, Ellie, Jenny, the Camden women, Jo, MohicAnne, Julie, Cherry and friend on motor bike, Anne-the-vicars-wife, who is so often there, plus masses of others. The main problem I had was women who came up to me and said "Hello Ginette" and, although I knew the faces, I could not put name to them. On Monday, Liz, Karen and two others came from Canterbury, so the whole weekend was a non-stop greeting of friends. Apart from these, other women came round from the other gates, so it was all quite exhausting.

Hilary and I had taken up a Gore-Tex, which had been given by special fund raising from Deal. I slept in it, and was strongly advised by the regulars to put my name on it so that it would not *'disappear'*. It would be used at Orange Gate by any woman who wanted it. It now has large red letters painted on it saying, "Ginette's, please return to Orange Gate Van". As soon as we arrived, we found Hilary, a Gore-Tex and set our sleeping things up in the rabbit meadow. There was, as usual, a very cold wind blowing round the campfire, but in the meadow it was warm and sheltered. As Lynne and co had to go back to Wales quite soon, we had a smoke and then I took them to the Oxford roundabout near Newbury, so they could hitch home.

Hilary and I had bought some Worthing mushrooms, and I had a load of purple sprouting from the garden, so I offered to cook supper. We had these with brown rice and onions and garlic, plus the odd bottle of wine to wash it all down. We sat round the fire for a while in the rabbit meadow, but as we were tired we went to bed quite early. It was a magnificent starlit night, and the nightingales were amazing. Hilary and I decided that there were at least two if not three of them. Earlier we had heard an owl, and in the dawn chorus, there was a cuckoo as well as the usual songbirds. As usual, I didn't sleep all that well that first night, but it didn't matter a bit. We were all rather concerned that Sian was ill. She had not been well for some days and was sleeping in the only tent in the rabbit meadow. She had had a temperature, and was very much under the weather, not feeling hungry, her eyes hurt (in the end I lent her my sunglasses). There was a sort of rule that we felt that tents were not appropriate in the rabbit meadow, so we just have the one 'sick bay' tent up there. The evening before Hilary had had a bad headache and one or two other did not feel that special. As it turned out it was not a good weekend health wise for Orange Gate. On the Saturday morning, just as I was about to get up I heard a scream from the campfire area then lots of voices. I did not get up immediately, but when I did and went round the fire I found Sally and Anne both had quite bad burns. I feel that I should have got up straight away and done something, as only the weekend before when I had been staying in Brixton, I heard a woman screaming, and did nothing about that either, except lie there and feel my blood run cold. What had happened at Greenham was that one of Margaret's cats had caught a little rabbit and Sally was trying to rescue it from its tormentor. She leant over the fire, her trousers caught alight, and she screamed and fell over and Anne put out the flames with her hand. The awful part was that Sally fell on the rabbit and killed it, but what was more concerning was that she had a nasty large burn on the front of her leg, and Anne had some nasty burns to her hand. They had put cold water on the burns, but Anne Francis and I decided that they needed treatment, so we went round in my car to Yellow, and hauled Sarah Hipperson out of her sleeping bag, to come and have a look. She is a trained nurse and after she had inspected the damage, was quite prepared to treat it, but had to have proper bandages and sterile dressings. She, Hilary and I went to Thatcham, got the stuff, and Sarah did an excellent job on dressing the painful and unpleasant burns. I took Sarah back to Yellow and came back for breakfast, at almost midday. Sally was very shocked and we persuaded her to lie down in the rabbit meadow and have an easy day.

It was so nice that in the end most of us ended up in the meadow, sitting, lying, dozing, reading, talking, feeding the invalids, smoking, drinking, etc. Some women came round from Green and told us that there was going to be a meeting about the action round the base the following afternoon. Hilary and I went off to see a friend at Green, and the meadow was full of little groups of women and children in varying degrees of dress and undress, enjoying the sun and cursing the clouds.

I have just realised that I am making myself sound even *more idle*, than I actually was. By the time I had been there 24 hours I had done two water runs and one wood run. The water collection was something I had always avoided before, and now I know why. Jill suddenly had a panic on Friday night when it was dark, that there was little water at Orange. Apart from drinking and cooking water, we are all very aware of fire hazard. We have had two fires near the campfire and rabbit meadow, both started, we are sure by vigilantes. The women put both of them out before too much damage was done, and before the fire brigade arrived, but the whole area is parched with masses of dead bracken and gorse all over the common. We have been warned many times by the fire officer about the danger and he says that fire can spread faster than we could run, so keeping a good supply of water is essential. The Friday night session was a fiasco! First, it took some time to locate the standpipe fittings, as we went to upstairs and of course, they were downstairs. We had all had a bit to drink and it was very dark. Jill drove us in the brown van, and to put it mildly we all got a little damp. In fact, I got bloody wet. The containers are very heavy and it is very hard to see when they are full, and the most likely way is when the water floods out of the top all over the woman holding it. The second time was slightly easier as it was daylight, but Anne's car got rather wet as we lost the lid of one container. Water runs are fine on a nice hot day, and without doubt not in *my* car! The wood collection was also essential. Although we had a certain amount hidden in the gorse for emergencies, we felt it would be good to go on to the common and collect enough for the weekend of timber lying around. Once again, Jill drove the brown van and Hilary, vicar's-wife-Anne and I went. Actually, this was very pleasant. It was really hot in the woods and there was plenty of timber just ready for burning. We got a huge pile and Jill had to drive back on her own while we walked, but it is amazing how quickly really dry wood does burn. On Sunday I did another of my horrible organising things, and asked everyone sitting round the fire to go and get an armful of wood. Actually most women did it quite happily as Sunday was a lousy cold day, and it warmed everyone up.

Saturday night at 8pm I produced my bottle of bubbly and about ten of us sat with our feet and legs in Sally and Anne's sleeping bags, drinking and celebrating Simone's wedding. Sian crawled out of the sick tent to be with us, and I was very conscious of Sally's burnt leg, which I tried not to touch. Ellen did a belly dance and luckily Cherry fairly early on had offered to go to the off-licence, so we had a whip round and three more large bottled of wine were consumed. There was a little crescent moon shining with the stars and nightingale was trilling in the distance. We all went to bed quite early again, and awoke to dull grey skies with a tiny bit of drizzle falling. It is quite OK in the Gore-Tex, but the getting up and dressed is not so easy in the wet, but I managed it and went for coffee.

Oh God, more trouble. Isia had brought her lovely cat Lucy with her, and unfortunately, someone had brought a dog to our camp and the cat and dog started fighting. Well, Isia tried to separate them and Lucy bit her hard on the hand. I had a look at it, and decided that Sarah was needed again. This time Rebekah came with Isia and me, and Sarah said that there was nothing she could do and that Isia must go to Basingstoke hospital, have it looked at properly and probably have a tetanus injection. I was going to take her, but Sally, Anne and Rebekah wanted to go and visit American Liz who was in there having just had her appendix out, so they all went.

At last, I got my breakfast, or was it lunch, I can't remember. Then much earlier than expected Ellie turned up. We found a good place to put the tent up, near where Jill sleeps. It was blowing about in the wind a bit, as the ground is so hard and stony it is difficult to get the pegs in firmly. Still it was a nice place, on bracken, which made it comfortable.

Some of us decided to go to the meeting at Green later. Hilary was very busy with Ruth and others gardening in the burnt area. They have cleared and dug the ground and are planting vegetables for use during the summer. In the end, I took Ellie, Maureen and Anne-the-vicars-wife. Jill went with Jay and another woman. The meeting took place in the middle of nowhere, so we could not be overheard. I saw Shirley from Faversham and also Canadian Stephanie, who decided to move to Orange the next day so I took all her gear back with me. The meeting very soon split into two, one group to have more action than the other. Jill and I decided that it would be better if those from Orange also split, so that we knew exactly what was going on. We must have been kidding ourselves, nobody knew anymore at the end than at the beginning. In my group of about 40 women, the only ones who had any idea of actions were Anne Frances and myself, so I'm afraid to say that between us we more or less took over the meeting. Everyone had their say. The general consensus was that we wanted to paint the fence, but if there was an area with individual woman, and it was swarming with cops, then we would not do anything. There seemed to be enough paint around, although Jill said she had some camp money to buy more if necessary. I am not even sure what the other group decided but I do know they split up again into smaller groups. It was all very typically Greenham, and in the end, I think everyone decided to do their own thing, but as far as possible, whatever this was, it should take place at 3pm.

Eventually we wandered back to Orange, and eventually got supper. There really was not much to be had unfortunately. What is happening is that visitors are not bringing nearly so much food as they used to because of evictions. There were one hell of many women staying, all wanting food. Jill and I ended up by eating out of the wok together. Some of us decided to go to the pub that evening for a drink for a change, and just as we were about to go, Christine turned up, and came with us. I took her and Ellie and Toni and Isia, Ellen and MohicAnne and Jill and Jay. We were chucked out of the first pub as Jay had been banned from it previously, so we went into Newbury and had a good evening there. I was careful not to drink too much as I was driving, but we took some cans back with us, and sat round the fire for a while. I showed Christine the Gore-Tex, and we all piled off to bed.

It was a very windy night, but at least the next day the sun was shining. I got up about 9 and took coffee back to the tent, and by the time we eventually surfaced, the whole of Orange Gate was swarming with day visitors, flying kites and generally wandering around.

More and more women turned up, and somehow I did not get breakfast until after 1.30. At Orange, we had decided amongst ourselves that we wanted to paint the gate its proper colour, so we all met with our pots, brushes, rollers, bits of rubber tied to sticks etc., all dressed in appropriate clothes, plastic bags, waterproof gear, hats (Ruth had a pair of knickers round her head) and marched firmly to the gate. Fantastic! The police just watched us. That nasty, rusty dull old gate was transformed. At one point, I remember being lifted onto Miranda and another woman's shoulders, and painting the top of it, and my brush was just the right size to poke through the mesh to paint the fastening. While all this was going on, other women were painting signs and symbols all over the road in a variety of colours. It was a good paint-drying day, and although we all got pretty well splattered, the paint was not too smudged by people walking over it. Then the police reinforcements came out. They made a couple of token arrests, and took away any pots and brushes that they could find lying around. On the whole, I don't think they were particularly worried by the action, but we all felt better for having done something positive.

Many of the visitors stayed round the gates singing, while the rest of us went back to the rabbit meadow. I had finished my two small pots of paint, so joined them there in the sun. We sat around for a while, talking and enjoying the sun again. Hilary and I decided to leave at about 6pm and take Cathy and Ellie back to London with us. We also thought we would have an Indian take-away in London, as there was still not a lot of food. We took the tent down, and started packing up the car, when suddenly, out from the gate came women in vans. They had cut their way in over on the north side, and had been caught, but the police were letting them out (they had painted symbols and slogans on the runway) without many arrests. Karen was in a hurry to get round to Violet, so I took her in the car, came back and said my farewells to everyone and the four of us left Greenham again. Sadly.

Another weekend full of friendship and incidents. I hope there will be no more accidents. They are frightening. It is still extraordinary how this world of mouth does work among the women. We had coach-loads at Orange. The police really do not know what we are going to do. We thought for a while we had a 'plant' put amongst us, but we were wrong. I would like to go to Brawdie for my birthday, but as yet, I am not sure if it is possible. The police are just as unpredictable as we are. When they released the women from the vans one copper suddenly called out a name. A woman came forward and he handed her a pen with her name on that she had dropped inside the base. A MoD policeman whom I had seen before, greeted me with "Hallo, you're here again are you? How are you keeping?" Cats and mice keep on playing these games, and the end is nowhere in sight.

30th May – 2nd June 1984

This trip to Greenham is vital. I had to recharge my batteries. I left my mother with lunch on the table and got to Orange Gate before two o'clock. The only women around were MohicAnne and Julie, wandering round eating breakfast/lunch. Jill was money woman for the week so she was at a meeting, Anne Frances, Reading Anne and Sally were in court, and Ruth appeared later that day. I never saw Anne the vicar's wife as she was sent to Holloway for 30 days, having refused to pay her fine on Christian principles. Reading Anne has a week in which to pay, so she organised with her bank to pay in 1p and 1/2p pieces. £75 in that sort of coinage takes a lot of counting!

The changes at Orange were mainly that the fire was back in its old place away from the trees, and there are no soldiers on duty at present. Instead, the MoD police are very much in evidence and some of them patrol with large Alsatian dogs. MohicAnne and Julie were rather concerned because the gate had been shut, and the rumour had gone round that cruise convoy was about to come out. At the moment Yellow is completely ballsed-up by the roadworks, and round Blue there are works again on every road in that area to do with drains, so the only possible gate to bring the convoy out is Orange, and it has been seen inside driving round. I said that I had seen what was happening and went round to Red where the women were sitting in the sun. Just as I was talking to them, '*Annabell*' with a load of women came round to say that all was quiet, the gates had been opened and they had been right round the base, so I returned to Orange, and got myself organised in the rabbit meadow with Gore-Tex and sleeping bags near Ann and Sally. We talked, read and dozed for a while, and I caught up on all the latest news. Sian and her hepatitis are much better, and she is having a holiday in Wales. The camp at Brawdie was a great success with lovely weather and lots of actions. Miranda is cycling back to Orange slowly along the coast, and Rebekah had to go straight to London. Anne gave me a lovely birthday card from Diana, and they all said they wished I had been with them in Wales. It was all quite quiet and peaceful, and the three other women who were in the tent packed up and left. We had supper and a jar of lemon curd and Julie and MohicAnne made, and a large bottled of my homemade elderberry wine, and drifted off to bed in good time.

The nightingale sang for me and the night was mild and fine. I didn't sleep very soundly, but felt peaceful although there seemed to be an enormous amount of traffic coming and going all night through the gate. At one time, I wondered if the night watch had gone to sleep as it sounded like huge vehicles on the moved, but I was too warm and comfortable to get up and find out. I had arranged with the night watch to call me just before they left, so they got me up at about 6.45and I went round to the fire. It was a bit of a mess round there, so I did a big wash-up and tidy-up before I had breakfast. Then, Reading Anne was up and ready to go to work. Julie and Jill were next up and I went off to phone my mother to check on her, and when I got back, Jill was off trying to organise the distribution of money round the gates. Sally, and Judy (from Indigo who had stayed the night) and MohicAnne were around, and we sat round the fire with cups of tea and coffee and Sally started reading Paradise Lost aloud to us. (We are now known as the cultural gate!) Before long, the visitors started arriving. A minibus from Wales with Dot (who I'd last seen on the soaking water run) with her daughter who'd been arrested on the fence painting day, and was therefore in court that morning plus some other friends from Wales. We sat and talked and ate, and other cars and visitors arrived with wood etc. The bailiffs also came, took out rubbish and told us to move the large pile of wood which was very visible by the fire, to behind the trees, so that if the boss turned up, it would not be seen.

At one point, I went round to the rabbit meadow for a few minutes, and when I came back, all the women were very worried. It appeared that five women from Hereford had got out of their car and were walking by the fence. One woman stopped and put her hands on it, and at that moment a MoD policeman, obviously off duty as he had an anorak over his uniform came up to her and said that she was tampering with the fence and he was arresting her for criminal intent. She protested, and her friend stepped forward to check the number on the policeman's shoulder under the anorak, and he grabbed her and said he was arresting her for assault. He took them both inside and of course, their friends were frantic. Everyone rushed up to the gate but got no help there, and eventually the women were taken off inside to Yellow to the interrogation room. Hours later, their friends were still looking for them, and we never heard what happened in the end. This is typical Greenham Common for you. Women walk round the fence, touch it, pull it, cut it, and nothing happens, but suddenly, bang, a woman get arrested for doing nothing at all.

When Jill came back she and I decided to go and find out about an old white van, which had been impounded some weeks before and was still in the pound, but we felt it would be worthwhile to get it out and use it as a store for eviction times. We gave MohicAnne a lift to the Oxford roundabout, as she had to go home to sign on, and eventually found the pound, in of course, Pound Lane. First Jill tried to get in the wrong vehicle, but in the end, we located the right one, which was decidedly tatty, with no tax disc or battery. We arranged to see the boss man the next morning about recovering it, but in the end, we found that the tax disc had probably been sent back for a refund and the vehicle was not insured, so we left it for the time being.

Back at Orange Reading Anne was back, Ruth was digging a shit pit (most necessary) so Anne and I did a water run in Mabel. We did not get nearly so wet this time, but those containers are damn heavy. My aching shoulder served me right for trying to keep up with Anne; she is *much* younger and stronger than I am!

I cooked supper for the seven of us, Anne, Sally, Ruth, Julie, Judy and Jill, of sea spinach from Brawdie, and scrambled eggs and cheese on toast. We sat and hoped that a night watch would turn up. It did not, so in the end, Judy and Ruth did the first turn and then Jill and I took over at 3.30. At about a quarter to two I was aware that the rain was starting, so I zipped up the hood of the Gore-Tex, but I couldn't make myself close it up completely. It brought back terrible memories of when I was a small child and my sister would pull all the bed covers over me and sit on me. I thought I was suffocating. A terrible sensation. Anyway, the Gore-Tex was fine, but its bloody hard to get out and dressed in the rain without getting wet, but I managed it, and drank my orange juice, put on my woolly hat and sat by the fire with an eiderdown over my legs, a roaring fire and a huge golf umbrella over me. Jill laughed like hell when she saw me and went for her camera, but she was very glad of the shelter, and in the end it was Reading Anne who laughed at us. Some of the vehicle drivers going in and out, turned, and looked at us. Jill and I sat there drinking coffee, and smoking, until 9am, we never drew breath; we just talked, and hardly noticed when it got light. Mind you, it was such a wet drab morning that even at nine o'clock it was not that light. It rained all morning, and after various chores Jill and felt it was time to get a bit of rest. I had a kip in the car and Jill in her sleeping area under a piece of plastic. Julie got us up at about 1 o'clock, as we wanted to go to a meeting at Green. I made a bit of soup and Judy came with us. Julie went to have a bath with a woman who turned up with all the essentials we wanted plus a Guardian and the offer of a bath. There are some marvellous women around. That is just the sort of support we need. We drove rounds to Green in a bad thunderstorm with the roads awash, but by the time we arrived it had almost stopped, so we sat in the clearing and the amazing meeting started.

The essence of the meeting was to *plan the start of the revolution!* A new experience for me, and I think for the others as well. Some of the women felt and feel that we have been at Greenham for a long time, we have had some fantastic demonstrations and support with 35,000 women turning up to circle the fence and to pull and cut the fence on other occasions. But, the media are more or less ignoring us, many people in this country think there are no longer women at Greenham, the cruise missiles are in, and more are coming, and there is no way we can stop them. There are just not enough of us. At Easter, it was estimated that about one million women turned out locally at the American bases throughout the country, but the news coverage was minimal. Many of the long-term residents at Greenham are quite convinced that the nuclear accident/war will take place within a year or so unless something dramatic is done to stop it. No more peaceful picnic-type demos or even fence damaging parties, but something so big that the country will *grind to a halt.* What we want is for ten million women to come to Greenham (or as near as they can get) for ten days from the 20th to 30th September. As we said, it is a women's strike and the start of the revolution in this country. *Wow!* The way to get this ten million is a bit like a chain letter.

Each of us will contact ten other women and persuade, cajole, insist, plead, etc. that they come, and these ten must do the same to ten others. This only needs to be done six times to get ten million women moving. Without doubt, the country will grind to a halt. We want the men to be supportive and look after children, older people etc., and keep the essential services going. Each woman would have to be self-sufficient for her time at Greenham, and there will be enormous problems over water, food, shit-pits etc., but we all feel that it is possible. Whether we will get ten million is academic, who the hell is going to count that number anyway? We also want women from Europe and the rest of the world to come. We are not asking working women to have their holiday leave at that time, but to just not go to work for those days. If there are enough prepared to do this, there is no question that they will get the sack, as work all over the country will stop. There just will not be enough people free to do it and the men will have to look after the children anyway. There are the usual reasons for not having men being actively involved with us, but their support is essential. If the authorities stop women at the ports, for example, the women will just have to jam the ports, or where they are stopped, and disrupt everything at the place where they are.

We sat and talked about this for some time and everyone had a chance to give her opinion. I did say that I thought ten days was a long time and would rather have about 5 days, but the general consensus was that to have a real impact, 5 days was not enough. Rebecca Johnson reminded is of the Lysistrata story of the women of Athens, and said that they must have had their problems just as much as women today. We had to think big to make this work at all. Jane Denning said the same and the rest of us agreed. We then sat and discussed what sort of leaflet should be produced (by the next day) for Jane to take to Speakers Corner as she was talking at an anti-apartheid rally in Hyde Park, and she wanted to have something prepared to talk about and have leaflets to hand out. We all had a chance to put forward our ideas, and it was hard not to sound like an advert. In the end we agreed unanimously that whatever the poster of leaflet said, it should be put under the heading "**Ten Million Women – Ten Days**".

We all felt that this huge gathering should not just be about the nuclear issue, but women's struggles for many things. There would be posters against rape, the colour question, and we must appeal to oppressed women of all types. We felt that if possible children should not be brought to Greenham at this time. As I have already said, it would be no picnic, and violence could well come from the authorities though fear of that vast number of women. We envisaged cars parked for miles up the M4 and all round Newbury as women tried to get as close as they could to be base. Everything would stop. We did not have time to discuss what actions should take place or any details; this was just a meeting to get the idea started, out of the women's heads on to paper.

Lisa has been making notes of all the comments under the shelter of my umbrella during the showers, and we left half a dozen women to put these notes into some sort of order for the leaflet. Apart from anything else, the following day was the first Saturday in the month when visitors are encouraged to come and visit the camps at Greenham and we wanted to be able to hand out information to then when we came. Two thousand leaflets had been prepared, printed and handed round each gate by 11am the next morning, so it just shows what Greenham women can do if they put their mind to it.

Jill, Judy and I staggered back to Orange in a state of euphoria and shock. We told the others what had happened, and spent a lot of time discussing it. The other women could see a mass of problems, but in essence, they agreed that it *will* take place.

As the evening wore on, more women arrived for the weekend, Isia, Lucy and others from London, Jane and a friend from Kent. Then the Friday night watch, Lyn and her friends who had found in a wood an abandoned night watchman's red and white striped hut, which they proceeded to put up. It is marvellous and really cheers the campfire area up. There was plenty of wood and some wine and food, so we settled in for the evening. There were a few women who had come for the first time, Hilary with her little dog, just for a night watch and Charlie from Germany. It is nice to know that newcomers do realise we are still here. I thought that the weather was still rather doubtful, so put my sleeping bag and Gore-Tex next to Jill under the plastic sheet she had strung up. We went to bed quite early as we were both very tired having been up at 3.30 that morning. It did rain in the night, and I pulled the plastic a bit more over us, but Jill had not heard either the rain or me moving around. I suppose if I stayed long enough I would sleep as deeply as that, but it takes a while to get used to being outside, and I am not there long enough.

I got up at about 9.30am and brought Jill a cup of tea in bed, but I had some phone calls to make. One was to check on my mother. The phone tapper must have had rather a shock as most of our discussion was about her piles, and I told her she "must use the suppositories" and how to deal with them! I arranged to be in London by about 6 o'clock that evening, and had already said that I would pick Karen up from Indigo and take her with me. In the end, I took Lisa and Kim from Green as well and it was good to have a car full.

We had a good tidy up and washed everything in disinfectant, as we are still being rather careful because of the hepatitis. Apart from

Sian, Hanna had it and Jane from Orange has been poorly and away from us for a little while.

The visitors arrived all day. I gave an interview to a Swedish journalist, talked to a German one, some Dutch Labour Party men and women, Quakers from Canterbury and Herne Bay, etc. It is lovely to see so many people supporting us, but it does make the residents tired to talk and answer the same questions all the time. We handed out masses of the Ten Million Women leaflets, and most people were enthusiastic. They agreed to have the leaflet duplicated and would pass it round to their friends. It was a start and things will build up from there, I know. Reading Anne was painting Mabel rose pink and I helped her.

While all this was going on, Jill was talking to two Irish women who had stayed for a while at Orange and came back for their dole money. We are very short of funds indeed at Greenham now, and some of this money had been allocated to other urgent needs, but it wasn't just the money that was the problem, but the fact that these women felt they weren't made really welcome at Greenham because they were working class and didn't fit in with the middle class women. This is a hell of a problem. We all feel that there are not enough working class women at Greenham, but now to encourage them is very hard. We were horrified to think that they felt they had been rejected by us, and it is something we must try to sort out. They feel we are superior, use words they do not understand and even the fact that some women drink herb tea and eat odd food, (vegans and vegetarians are numerous) makes some of these other women feel like outsiders. Other women have told me that they think Greenham is a middle class enclave and it is only those with a privileged background who have the security to be at Greenham, as if things go wrong, they can go back home if necessary. This subject has come up many times, and we are aware of it, but more effort on both side must be made for the inclusion of all women.

Just before 5 o'clock, I packed my things in the car, including the rest of the French marigolds. Some I had planted at Greenham in the flower garden, and the others I wanted to take to Mongeham. I said goodbye to my friends, picked up Karen from Indigo, and Lisa and Kim from Green. We got to London just before 7 o'clock.

28th June – 1st July 1984

I was going to go to Greenham on the 28th, but after a phone call from Sally at 2.30am on the 26th, I was even more determined that nothing would stop me. Sally phoned to tell me that the cruise convoy had gone out of Orange Gate an hour and a half earlier, and when I asked if she wanted me to come there and then, she said that was not why she had phoned, she just wanted to talk to a friendly Orange Gate woman. They had been pinned down by the police in the usual fashion, but Jill had managed at some point to get into her car, lock it, and park it firmly in front of the gates. It had not been possible to tow the car away, but eventually they had pushed it to another position, and then found that she had not locked the boot, so pulled all her possessions out, flung them into the bushes, and then pulled Jill out. She gave an interview to the Guardian the next day and on Wednesday, 'Lovejoy Peace' made the front page!

I played a foursome's golf match on Thursday morning (and won) before the long and tedious drive to Newbury, arriving in the middle of the afternoon. Ruth and Penni, Sally (Anne came later), MohicAnne, Jane, Margaret, Wendy from Devon, Joan and about an hour after my arrival, Miranda on her bike. During the next couple of days, some of these went and others arrived. Julie with a woman from Rugby with her two children, Isia and Lucy with Jan and Josie from Gravesend, Christine and her niece Samantha, a French Canadian woman called Lorraine, then Astrid with four Danish women plus the night watch women each night, plus others whose names I never got.

The fire was in the open and most of the women slept near the fire under the trees, as vigilantes had been wandering round the rabbit meadow a week or so ago, and the women were understandably frightened, especially when they found a tennis ball filled with paraffin, and a wick nearby. Jill's plastic cover was still in its usual place, and Jay suggested that I joined her that night, as Jill would not be there until the next night. We talked and exchanged news for a while, and then Wendy came steaming along in her car to tell us that the north side were being evicted. There were enough women to cope, although by this time it was nearly 5pm, and we really could not believe it would happen. We also had the hassle of the BBC film crew around doing a programme for Songs of Praise for some man who wanted some shots of Greenham camp as he sometime brought wood to the camps. We were getting a bit tired of being unpaid extras, and started *'camping'* up like mad and making a bloody nuisance of ourselves. In the middle of this the muncher arrived, so we rushed round and put everything in the vehicles, but funnily enough the film crew promptly put their cameras away, and sat in their cars while the eviction was going on. We all felt that those scenes would make an interesting Songs of Praise, but perhaps it was a bit too controversial. The day visitors and bailiffs and film crew left, and I got out the *dolmades* I had made and the wine, and we say and had an early snack before the main meal. Money is very short at Greenham now, and the food stocks are right down, but we managed to have a good meal. It was getting cold so we moved the fire back under the trees. The Brick Lane legless chair is really good and very much appreciated. The ten million women bowl is now in the crockery section, which is a huge pram.

Life after supper was not very peaceful. The rumours about the return of the cruise convoy started coming in. First, we built a barricade down the lane with wood, chairs, boxes, earth etc., etc., and cars, then Rebecca Johnson came in her car and Jay and I decided to go with her to Yellow, as that is where we thought the action would be. There were many women there, all milling around waiting for something to happen. Sightings had been made only a few miles away, so the women decided to block the roadway to the gate with a fire made on a pallet, and dragged into position. More fuel was hurled on it and quite a blaze started. The police came along and tried to put it out, and then the fire engine came. Rebecca, Jay and I hid behind the bus shelter over the road, as we knew that the police would surround the women as soon as the convoy was close, and we thought we would escape notice there. Well, we stayed, crouched down there for some time, and nothing more was happening, so Jay and I decided to walk back to Orange along the fence. This was the only occasion when I was glad to have the perimeter lights, as the going is very rough, and in places incredibly swampy, and you have to pick your way over bits of wood, and other woman-made bridges, otherwise you end up ankle deep in rusty coloured slime. It took me half an hour of brisk walking and Jay ran on ahead.

Women at Orange were just sitting around waiting. We wondered if the whole thing had been a false alarm, and as it was about 1.45am we decided to go to bed. I had just taken off my shoes and trousers and crawled into my sleeping bag, when Jay shouted that something was about to happen. She had seen a lot of soldiers at the gate looking intently down the road. Someone had heard that it was definitely coming in at Yellow, so Ruth, Joan, Jane and I leapt into the brown van and shot round in that direction. When we reached the main Basingstoke road we were blocked by the police, so we turned the van round and drove back until we found a turning, which we thought, would wind back towards the fence and Yellow gate. Well, it did come back to the fence, but it was miles to Yellow and once again, that evening I found myself floundering through the swamp!

By the time, we got to Yellow the bloody convoy was back inside. What had happened was that the last of the four huge vehicles had broken down a hundred yards from the gate, and one of the other lorries had backed out from the gate and towed it back in. Only two women had got close to the convoy and they has been caught by the police and taken inside. We heard that they had been taken to Newbury nick, so Jay & I went with Pip & another Red Gate woman and went there to give them support. 50 or 60 women turned up there and we keened for about 10 minutes. We certainly made a hell of a noise, and then Sarah Hipperson came out and told us that she and Rebecca Johnson had not been charged, and they were free to go. In the meantime, Jay and another woman had sprayed a feminist symbol on a police van, so we left and went back to Orange, with Joan who turned up, having last been sighted by my plunging through the swamp!

Back at Orange, quite a few women were wandering around, so we told them what had happened, and as it was now about 4am and getting quite light, decided to go to bed.

Although I was exhausted, I must have walked miles that day; I woke up quite early with this damn cough, and started another day.

Friday was a comparatively quiet day. We expected the bailiffs who never turned up. Visitors came and went, we tidied up. MohicAnne showed me her artwork that I thought was excellent. I phoned Somerset to contact my sister Gina and arranged that I would pick her up at Basingstoke station at 9am on Sunday. I took Ruth and Penni to the Newbury roundabout as they wanted to hitch to Wales, and I did a load of shopping in Thatcham, etc. Greenham is now very short of money indeed. There was £10 which I took for food, but spent a fair bit more, as we were very short of suppliers, but in the end we had a very good evening meal, cooked mainly by Wendy. Donations are just not coming in now and we have to keep enough money for petrol as well as food, to drive off in eviction time.

I heard a sad story about Blue Gate, who piled all their possessions in their can, then found they did not have a driver amongst them, so the bailiffs drove off with everything, except a saucepan of bean stew. They got most of it back, but it must have been terribly depressing. (Actually, they broke into the pound and stole it back that night.)

We talked a lot about the return of the convoy. We felt that the Orange Gate barricade had been good, but we had not been at all effectual about our own blockading, and there were plenty of women around. It is hard to know what else to do that is going to really work.

The Guildford night watch turned up, and a few of us decided to do a little decorating. Wendy and MohicAnne were the keenest, plus Julie and Jane and myself. Half way to the area, where we were going in I suddenly decided not to continue. I'm really not sure why. It just didn't feel right for me. I wasn't frightened or terribly tired or anything constructive like that, but I just thought that that particular night was wrong. We stopped and I told the others and Jane agreed that she didn't really want to go into the base either, so we turned back. Nobody worried; the others just went on without us. I am glad to say they had a very successful time, and now one of the watchtowers is a very pretty *geranium* colour.

I went to bed at about 1am, but it was not a good night for us. Julie had decided to sleep where the benders used to be on MoD land right by the fence. I am not sure if this sparked off the disturbance during the night, but the soldiers shouted and banged and yelled and carried on about every 20 minutes during the night. Julie eventually gave up and came to the rabbit meadow, having had stones thrown at her. At one point, the noise was so dreadful that I got out of my sleeping bag and Gore-Tex, put on my trousers, and went to the campfire to find out *what the hell* was happening. It was just the soldiers being bloody awful but they certainly succeeded in keeping most of us awake.

Saturday was a much nicer day. The wind was not nearly as strong and the sun shone most of the time. The dust at Orange is everywhere. It blows around all the time, and your feet get foul in no time at all, as well as the rest of you. At least it is a lot easier to wash properly, and the water in containers warms up slightly in the sunshine, so that you only need a small amount of kettle water for extra heat. I tried to make various phone calls, all abortive, and eventually found that Ellie would not be coming, as she had to work.

I was still feeling rather tired, so Wendy and I decided to sunbathe and doze in the rabbit meadow. Well we certainly sunbathed, but got no sleep and we talked for ages, then Christine and Samantha (plus beer, cider and wine turned up), then Isia, Jan and Jose, so although it was a relaxing time I didn't get a chance to read even a single line of my book. Eventually hunger made us active again, and some of us decided to do a tour of the gates and buy some more booze for the evening. We had a pleasant tour round, and found there were quite a lot of women at most of the gates, but Indigo had only two, so we promised to send more to support them. Back at Orange, the place was buzzing. Astrid and her five Danish friends were there, plus night watch and others. A marvellous meal was ready. There were five different salads and three hot dishes. It really was a splendid meal. Then Astrid produced a bottle of rum to go in the coffee, and then a bottle of scotch appeared. We all sang Greenham songs and danced around. We made so much noise that two women from Red Gate heard us and came round to join us. There were 24 women round the fire that evening, and we had a great time.

As the painting session had been so successful the night before, we decided to try again. We had previously checked that the paint pots and brushes were still hidden in the bushes, so Wendy, Lorraine, Jan and Jose and I decided that we would continue the brightening up of the base. We had seen some blue vans, and thought they would be much nicer with some decorations. The cutting went like a dream. My bolt cutters are great. First, the fence, then the barbed wire, then across the path and more barbed wire. Somewhere, I must have cut myself as my hand was covered in blood, but I never discovered when or where. Once inside we crept up a path and stood in a little copse of trees and bushes to decide what to do next. We heard a vehicle driving round and crouched down. We didn't hear it go away, and stood silently for a while. Then I started to cough. This was not fair on the others, so I said I would go back to the camp and they could carry on without the extra hazard of one member of the party coughing every few seconds. I retraced my steps and went back to Orange without any trouble. I went to bed, and it was not until the next morning that I heard what had happened to the others.

The authorities have now decided that they no longer want soldiers or police to patrol on foot but they drive round the base, and quite often just sit in a car and wait for something to happen.

Anyway, the four women started painting, heard a noise and dived for the bushes. They were lying there when they heard a man's voice telling them to stay still until he had *'Toto the dog'* under control. They had no intention of moving, when they heard this. (Lorraine was watching a shooting star with fascination anyway.) The police took them in the van to the interrogation room at Yellow. They kept them there for an hour or so. At one point, the women heard over a police walkie-talkie that they had seen me and gave a description, including that my bolt cutters were *"shining"*. That was clever of them as the cutters are dark coloured and are not shiny! The women were released at Blue Gate and were given a lift back to Orange by the night watch.

Overall, the police are not too keen to charge women. I think they just want to stop us getting in and out of the base at will, and it all costs too much in court cases and prison sentences. The security there is very low key at present. Di McDonald even drove her Dormobile in through Yellow Gate this weekend, and other women have cycled in the base in broad daylight before being caught.

I had to get up quite early again to meet Gina, and then brought her back for a coffee and she met some of my Greenham friends. She stayed there for a couple of hours with me, and then I said my goodbyes. I left Reading Anne making an inspection pit for pink Mabel. I thanked Astrid for giving me the excellent photos, and drove Gina round the north side to show her some of the other camps. I collected the towrope I had lent to Blue Gate to haul a door up a tree to make a tree house, picked up a woman who wanted to go to Indigo urgently, and drove to London.

When I got home, I found a post card from Cleis waiting for me. She is on holiday in Sark, but I know we will meet up again soon at Orange Gate.

Under 48 hours after cutting fence and barbed wire at Greenham, I had to use the bolt cutters again for quite another use. Under the eyes of a Royal Marine, I had to cut a very loose shoe off Domino, a horse. Everyone thought that the cutters were a useful tool to keep in the car, but I did not let on what I usually used them for.

I sent Lovejoy Peace the Guardian cutting about her. I hope she gets it safely, as although I sent it to Orange Gate, I know that she is now living *inside* the base for as long as she can.

23rd – 31st July 1984

The rabbit meadow is quiet and hot with Ulla writing-up her diary and the other women round the fire drinking coffee and eating toast with jam or peanut butter, but no marge or ordinary butter as there is none and we are pretty broke. I have just had a complete body wash and feel almost human, although still quite tired. Yesterday was long, and I feel I must write it up before we are evicted, or they bring cruise back in again, or I just fall asleep.

When I arrived yesterday morning, Orange Gate was quiet with just a few women around. Ruth and Penni were just off to Wales for an all-women's picket in support of the miners, and the other regulars still here are Jane, MohicAnne, Jill and Jay (still in bed) Hannah, Helen whom I seen at other gates, and Ulla and French Fredric. I had a coffee then went and woke Jill and Jay, as I wanted to hear about their time at *"Nettle Camp"* inside the base. It had been a great success. Rebecca brought them provisions every night and kept the press informed, and they just stayed (quietly) all the time. When the rain started, they put up a polythene shelter, and kept a low profile when the patrol vehicles went round. What was amazing was that when Tony Benn leaked in the House of Commons that two women were living in the base, patrols were sent out to search for *'Julia'* and *'Kate'*, and at one time the soldiers with torches were only eight yards from them and their shelter and they were sure they would be discovered. The soldiers went away. The next day Jill & Jan had to walk quite a long way to find someone to give themselves up to, as everyone was still looking for them. They had fun wandering round and inside buildings before they were finally arrested. None of the authorities believed that they had lived at Nettle Camp for a week, so the women suggested that a *shit count* should be taken. The British MoD police were not too keen on this idea, but the Americans did discuss that an "excrement patrol" might be used to dig up this vital evidence. Jill and Jay were let out without being charged and gave interviews in the press, then had a fantastic party, which appears to have been very memorable! I do not think this is the last we shall hear of Julia and Kate, somehow I think they have more schemes up their sleeves or armpits.

Back at the fire, people were arriving. The two women who had been arrested just for walking along by the fence has been in court in the morning, and also the Welsh crowd, Dot, Kay & co who were done for painting the road on the gate painting day. They all had fines and seven days to pay them, but I do not think they were in any hurry to comply with the law. We sat round and talked and then the Welsh took Ruth and Penni back with them. Jane, Ulla and I went shopping in Thatcham. Then, we went round to Red where we saw Lorraine who lives there now, with Karen from Merseyside, and others. There was a general feeling that we were all ready for a little action that night, but we would see how it all went and Jane and I offered to do night watch for the first part of the night then Jill and Jay would take over from us. We had a huge supper of mixed salad, a ratatouille with Worthing mushrooms, and hummus made by Jane. There was a strong aroma of garlic round us after this, and then Jill produced redcurrants and custard for pudding. We had a homemade wine given by the Welsh and the elderberry I had brought with me, but neither Hannah nor Jane could drink until Christmas because of the hepatitis they have both had.

Women drifted off to bed and Jane and I sat by the fire as it was quite a cool night with the wind blowing round us, and the CB radio tucked in Jane's boot. We were in the middle of a long intellectual (ha ha) conversation at about 1am when the CB made a strange noise, and Jane heard that the cruise convoy had just been taken out of Yellow Gate. We woke everyone up and, as we learnt that it had headed down the road in the direction of Newbury, we thought it was worth a try to find it in my car. We stopped at Yellow where a few women were wandering rather unhappily around, and then shot off in the M4 direction. I had to get more petrol in my car, and when we reached the main roundabout, decided it was no good just chasing after something that might not be there, so came back home via Blue, to check whether they knew about it, then Yellow for more news. Nothing was happening, so we went back to Orange where we saw Karen who had just been let out of the Gate, having literally walked into the base at Indigo gate as they had lost the padlock! Hannah, Helen, Jane and I decided to do some cutting down near the end of the runway. When we came near the fence from round the back path, we thought we saw vehicle lights on the runway, so Hannah and I decided to go on and find out what we could. The lights were just a figment of our imagination, an optical illusion. Right at the end of the runway there was a small rather unlit area of fence, so I waded in with the cutters. Quite quickly, I had a woman-sized hole, then Hanna took over and cut the barbed wire, then we went across the patrol path and cut the inner role of razor and barbed wire. We then went back to the others, had a coffee and a chat, and decided to go in down the runway and get as close as we could to Yellow to cheer up the women there. Karen came with us.

Well, we were accompanied to the hole by the barking guard dogs from the wood yard, which were noisy enough to waken the entire base, but there was no one around and we went inside through all the holes on to the runway. We walked up it hand in hand and every time we saw a vehicle driving round the road, we fell flat on our faces until it passed. Unfortunately by this time it was starting to get light with a beautiful pink sky, so we walked and danced along quite briskly, getting bolder all the time. We must have walked for about an hour, passing one huge building on our left, and then we saw another building, a hanger I think, and decided we would go round behind it towards Yellow Gate. The cars were still patrolling round the road and it was really was light by now, and once we ran and ducked behind some private cars, then went along the building, round a corner, and I saw a truck with a man sitting in it. There was nothing we could do except walk past him and say *"Good morning"* politely, and then go on round the next corner. At this point six vehicles screamed up: three police & three US army, and more or less surrounded us. We did not take a lot of notice of them, but talked to two American soldiers in a truck with a very nasty looking machine gun on the seat between them. Eventually the police rounded us up, put Karen, Hannah and me in the back of one car, and Jane and Helen in the other. It appears their policemen asked them what they had had for supper, as the garlic smell was oozing from every pore by that time. In fact, I'm surprised they didn't smell, rather than see us in the end.

We were driven at a furious speed to the interrogation centre near Yellow Gate, and then processed one by one. We had already agreed that we were all called Jenny Williams and that we lived at the Peace Camp. Jenny Williams is the wife of an MoD policeman from the base, who has left her husband and lives with us. She had had reporter trouble, so was more than happy that we should use her name. I was taken off first to be searched. I had previously been told that I was arrested for suspicion of criminal intent, and the usual guff about not having to say anything, but if I did, etc. I was taken to the Ladies, and the first thing I saw was a washbasin and mirror. I looked filthy so before the policewoman could stop me I started having a good wash, my hands, then my face, both of which seemed to have a lot of runway dirt adhering. She was very cross and told me to hurry up. She then told me to take off my sweaters and undo the top button of my trousers and then she gave me a quick rub down. (The cutters were safely back in the car, of course.) She took away my cigarettes, lighter & car keys and put them in a bag. She asked my name. I said "Jenny Williams, date of birth 28.4.33, place of birth, Chalfont St Peter". God, I thought I was a truthful person! The sergeant took me to the interrogation room, where he asked once again: my name, date and place of birth. I gave the same wrong information, and then to every other question, I said no comment, or refused to answer. He pretended to show some surprise when I refused to rise to this question of why I broke into the base, but I thought being completely non-committal would speed things up, and the others could have a go if they wanted to. After all this was my first arrest. You need practice at this game. I then had to sit down on the floor outside the office away from the others, while they went through the same process. We were not with him more than about 2 minutes each, and the others were looked after by a young copper called Oliver who was much friendlier and more relaxed, except when Hannah and Jane very theatrically pretended to be in love, when he looked resolutely out of the window. When Karen was finally finished with, the sergeant came out to us all sprawled on the floor and said that we were very lucky not to be charged (mind you they hadn't a leg to stand on as they had no evidence as to how we got in and we all given different ways or said nothing). We were escorted to the Gate, said out farewells to Oliver and left.

We thought that Yellow Gate women would be glad to see us, but there was no one in sight, they had all gone to bed and the fire was out! We made it up had some foul coffee and tea without milk, and by this time a car turned up with a CND peace group searching for the convoy, then Jill, Jay and Carola appeared across the road where they had been hiding in wait for the convoy to return and we all got lifts back home. By this time, it was 7am, so I had some toast and went to bed in the rabbit meadow. I got up about 11am and now that it is something after 3pm, think it is time to get some more sleep. Today could be as long as yesterday.

The rest of Tuesday was comparatively quiet. We had many visitors with food and sympathy, but among the women who were here during the night was a feeling of restlessness because the convoy was out, and tiredness through lack of sleep. We all drank a lot of coffee and tea and picked at food continually. It really was one of those days when it would be impossible to answer the question, what do you do at Greenham all day, with any sort of rationality. About six times I thought I would wander off and have a quiet read or sleep, but each time I was about to do so, someone else would turn up, and the conversation got interesting. There is also an awful lot of walking up and down the road, deciding that the washing up does need doing, we must get some more wood for the fire, or the kettle needs filling and boiling, or vegetables need chopping for the evening meal. When I did get round to the rabbit meadow, MohicAnne came and showed me her poetry and we had a long talk. She was sparkling fit and wide awake as she had managed to sleep through most of the night on the mattress by the fire, even when we firmly woke her and asked her to finish the night watch at about 7am, she said yes she would, then fell fast asleep until 10am. She has a great capacity for food and sleep, as well as writing interesting and perceptive poems.

We decided that we must prepare material for a blockade at the end of the road in case they bring the convoy back by our gate, and at about 10pm Jay, Jill, MohicAnne and I went to the pub for a swift drink. Our reception there was not particularly friendly from the locals, and although it was not very warm, we preferred to take our drinks outside. At least I had a good wash in the loo in hot water, and when we came back, we found the women had filled all the bags with soil for the blockade, and dumped them in the ditch, so we went to bed. At some time in the evening, Jay and MohicAnne had cut a bit of the gate so that we could get the Citadel lock on it, and MohicAnne sat on her blankets near me practicing with the key to make it work as efficiently as possible.

The next thing I knew was that I was being woken by rain falling on my face. I then had this usual problem of whether it was better to get wet, or to suffocate. I found I had to leave a tiny breathing gap, so the rain collected in a puddle near the hole, and then poured in down my back! Not very comfortable, but I dozed. I woke with a start when it was light to a shout from MohicAnne "Fuckin' hell". She had no Gore-Tex and had been getting wetter and wetter in her blankets for well over an hour. She disappeared, and I tried to sleep again, but was quite glad to get up at about half past seven, when the rain eased a little, get dressed and go round to the fire. The women, MohicAnne and the night watch, had moved the fire under the trees, and put the shelter up, so we huddled under that most of the morning. Luckily, we had plenty of food and water, so apart from visits to the shit pits and cars, we stayed fairly dry. Once again, I thought I would have read, but only managed a few pages.

As it was Wednesday there was a money meeting at Red, and I arranged that I would take Hannah and Helen to the roundabout, then some visitors turned up and said they would take them. Ulla wanted to go to the bank, and we suddenly realised that Jill should go to the money meeting, so once again I woke her. It appears that she and Jay had not got to bed until very late, as they had been collecting barbed wire for the blockade and making 'cat flap' holes in the fence. The idea of these if that it would save a lot of time and walking if we have cat flaps near each gate, then we can go visiting other gates by taking a short cut through the base, rather than going round it. Anyway, Jill had camp money so decided to go to the meeting and as she had this cash and didn't want to be pressurised by other women, got dressed in her 'heaviest' clothes, and Ulla and I put on leather jackets, and I made a rollie for each of us. The heavy mob was certainly in town, but Jane spoiled the image with a skirt on! It was still raining, so once we had made our dramatic entrance I got the golf umbrella for Jill to have a dry spot to enter in the money book, dole names for each gate, food and petrol money and general requests. The meeting was very quiet and successful, mainly because after the essentials, which came to over £1,000, there was only a couple of hundred left for the requests and these were quickly agreed on. The general consensus was very sensibly that top priority for money must go to women to pay fines for those who could not go to prison.

The meeting only took about an hour, so I drove Ulla, Jane and Nicki to Thatcham; we did some shopping and came home. I was about to go and have a quiet read when a familiar roaring noise told us that Mabel, pink and beautiful as ever, had brought Anne and Sally back and Ruth also, after the women's picket for the miners in Wales. We exchanged news, and after a while made a start on the wine Ulla had bought as she is leaving on Friday, and got supper ready. We also heard that there was a lot of activity at Tidworth on Salisbury Plain where the convoy was, so it was more than likely it would come out tonight. Anne thought it would be a good idea if we checked with Eileen, so MohicAnne, Barbara (who wanted a lift to Yellow) and I went to Eileen's house. It was very dark along there, but Eileen confirmed the activity reports on her CB and we went back to Orange. The barricade was being put up, so I helped with that. We found the stashed barbed wire and the road works flashing light, which we placed on top. By this time, many women were around, so another campfire was put near the corner so that women could see if any car lights came down the road. The convoy was still in Tidworth according to the CB, so I went to bed. After about half an hour, I was called out of my *pro tem* and rather wet bender, which I had constructed earlier in case it bucketed down again that night, and went to see what was happening. (Actually, I went to bed twice that night and was woken up again, but I cannot remember what took place on the previous occasion).

Anyway, the cruise convoy was back inside, at Blue Gate this time. I am still not sure quite what happened, as it appears there was a good barricade, but with about four active women. Everyone was very upset, just standing around in small groups. On the way there, we had passed about ten police vans. By the time we got back to Orange, they had dismantled our blockade and the one at Yellow. Karen, MohicAnne and some others from Red felt they wanted to go inside so I said I would help cut and then hide the cutters and go to bed. We had previously seen where only a few cuts were needed, so Karen and I started, but this place was very bright, and right at the end of the internal road, which was very busy with base traffic. I felt it was stupid to go on cutting there, so we all went back to Orange, and I went to bed.

By this time, it was once again getting light, so I pulled my sleeping things out from under the polythene, and as it got hotter stripped off more and more clothes and ended on top of the Gore-Tex at about 8.30. Jill is off to Peru for 3 weeks so she came and said goodbye, and I have just had coffee and a bath. It is steaming hot here in the rabbit meadow, and about time I was sociable again. God, I have just checked it is nearly 1 o'clock. Good, lunchtime.

26th – 31st July 1984

The rest of Thursday was pretty quiet. We had various post mortems as to why and how the convoy got back so easily and there was a non-violence workshop at Orange, but I decided to have a quiet afternoon and a read in the sun. Ulla was there, but we didn't talk much. She did say that she had never been to an English pub, so after supper Reading Anne, Sally, Jane, Ulla and I went to the Rockaby. I am not sure that it is a typical pub, as it is Irish, very noisy and is the only pub in Newbury who accept Greenham women. Anyway we had a beer there and then came back home where Dot, Kay et al from Wales had come to do night watch and have a chat. We talked to them for an hour or so, I read what I had written about this week, MohicAnne read some poetry, and then we went off to bed. I have moved into Jill and Jay's shelter, although I don't think it is going to rain.

Friday morning I was up in good time, as I had promised Ulla I would take her to Newbury station, and Sally wanted some new shoes. We did not spend long there, but it really was a relief to get back to Orange and peace and quiet. All week we have had a steady flow of visits, sometimes women from other gates, but also outsiders, who bring food, drink and wood, and want a chat. It is amazing how much time this takes, and there is such a variety of both men and women. Religious, usually Quaker, an Indian woman who is a great believer in Ghandi non-violence methods of peace, Germans, Scandinavians, Dutch, etc. Some come on bikes, some in cars, and others walk from the station or coach stop. We get gifts of lovely things like grapes, or basics like bread and lentils and fruit juice. We all drink a fantastic amount of fruit juice in this hot weather, and in Newbury I bought 5 cartons, which were drunk by half a dozen women in a few hours.

In the early evening Anne, Sally and I walked down to Eileen's to get the battery recharged for the CB, and had a cup of peppermint tea, saw the kittens and horses, parrot, dogs and cats. She and her family are becoming more and more supportive. Back at the camp, we had a couple of beers and supper, and then I met Ellie off the coach. We had decided to do part of the Ridgeway walk the next day, and in the end walked from 1.30 to 8.30, then had an Indian meal in Wantage, (having gone into and then crept out of a rather expensive and too smooth French restaurant). I did not have a very good night, as at some time during it I heard a rustling, then *"Hello, its Jay here. I'm back. Its quarter to four.*" Well, I wasn't feeling terribly chatty, although I was in her home. Then an hour or so later I had terrible guts ache, so went for a walk up the road, then sat by the dead fire for a while. There was no night watch, and there were so few residents that everyone felt it was unlikely that another convoy would be brought out, particularly on a Saturday night. Reading Anne appeared, just as I was starting to feel human again, so I left her making up the fire, and went back to bed where I dozed for hours. By the time we got up, Margaret, Sally and Anne, and American Liz and Toni who had both just come for the night had gone, but Maureen was there. Frederic had gone home to France, and Ruth & Jane were going to Emerald Gate, so we were very thin on the ground. We sat and talked for a while, and then Maureen Ellie and I decided to take some water round to Emerald. We parked at Green and walked with our water containers. It was the first time any of us had been there, and it is lovely, miles from any road, but lots of trees and heather all around. The camp is there as it is the nearest point along the fence to the silos, and the women can keep a close eye on what is happening. Each time a silo door is opened an alarm system goes off, so the security really is tight, although there did not seem to be many soldiers on guard. Although there is no gate at Emerald, it is good to know that women can give the rest of us warning if there is unusual activity inside.

We walked back to Green, then drove round the other gates and stopped at Red. Lorraine gave us some salad vegetables as we are short of them. Later she came round to us for some cooking oil and had a swig of our rum! I took Ellie to the coach stop and came back to find two German men there with Maureen and American Susan. They asked if they could cook and eat with us, and we agreed, but told them that no men were allowed around after dark. Maureen and I took the battery to be recharged, leaving the men cooking (that makes a change) and by the time we got back food was ready. Susan had a salad, and I made some dressing for it. It was a good meal, and they also left us most of a bottle of rum when they left.

I should mention on our way to Eileen's I met Di McDonald whom I had not seen for ages. We had a talk and she told me about a march to Dungeness Power Station next month, and gave me the name of a contact in Brighton. I will try to get some women from Deal involved. Di's van looked battered, and I am not surprised. Since I last saw her she had been involved in so many actions, I can understand why I can never make contact with her. On one she was being harassed by tanks in front and behind and a helicopter bouncing on and off the roof of her van! She really is an amazing woman. A woman also from Southampton told a hair-raising story about trying to find contacts. The first three phone booths were out of order and when she got to another one and was inside making a call, a tank with gun poised drew up outside the box with armed soldiers looking out of the turret. She finished her call, and in great fear went to her car and drove off. She was not followed or anything, this is a meant to be peaceful England and as she said, she pays her taxes to be defended by soldiers not to have them point guns at her from a tank!

In the end last night, Maureen, Sue and I were joined by potter Angie from Norfolk, then Jane came back, so we decided that I would have the CB and we would all sleep near the fire. Just as we were about to go to bed, Julie arrived with a bicycle and flat tyre. Anyhow, we all flaked out and slept within calling distance of each other. Maureen told us this morning that the cruising police had shown much interest in our night watchman's hut and long ladder found by Jane, so we have just stashed them in the bracken and tidied up ready for an eviction, which must come soon.

Monday really was a quiet day, apart from more visitors. We had a stream of them in the afternoon, all with exactly the same questions. The opening one is *"How long have you been here?"* And, the next one is *"What do you do all day?"* We had a long discussion among ourselves about this and decided that these questions were really quite logical, as the visitors wanted to talk to long-term residents, and not make fools of themselves by asking questions of other day visitors. The second question follows on, to get us to talk about ourselves and find out what makes us tick. In contrast to them, we do look pretty scruffy, we sleep in the open, we break the law by getting into the base, and perhaps most important of all, we are still at Greenham. Many of the visitors have gone to other gates, and have been slightly shocked (so they tell us) that at some gates the women are *'punk'* and sit on each other's laps!! There is no answer to these remarks, but we just remind the visitors that these women are at Greenham and that particularly on the North side, they have far more to put up with in the way of evictions and much more uncomfortable living conditions and lack of privacy than we do at Orange. Some visitors seem almost hostile, but they do come, and without their help, it would be harder for all of us to exist. Perhaps we are all there for our own personal reasons as well as cruise. I tried to explain at one time to some visitors about the enormous support we get from each other. That, for example, although I had lived in Deal for 20 years and knew masses of people, if I was in trouble or needed help, I knew that without doubt I could ask almost any woman from Greenham and she would give help without question, and gladly. There would be no excuses that she was *busy that day*, or *had relatives coming to stay*, or *a dinner party to organise*. She would just say, "*Yes, come*". There is a closeness, which is hard to explain to any outsider, we are safe and secure with each other, although there are no many differences between us. We can be ourselves, and are accepted as such. And, because of this we become stronger.

The expected evictions never came, although we had everything tidied up. Maureen even found a cheque and a £5 note in the food containers. The cheque was very wet, but still legible, dated March. We dried it and put it in the brown van. Orange Gate still has an account of its own and half the money goes still to oppressed and deserving women in the world. We did agree that the next amount should be sent to the Pacific Fund quite soon. Zohl will make sure it gets to the right source.

I still had stomach problems, so spent some time lying on the big mattress, taking it easy, but I did not feel like eating. Later in the afternoon Penni came back for the night from Wales with two women and Jodi. Then Jay and Barbara arrived to ask if we wanted to help in an action at Burghfield as they expected the Polaris missiles to be brought from Faslane and wanted to blockade them. They have observers all the way, and once it leaves Faslane, it should give us enough time to prepare a reception, no matter what route it takes. I said I was interested and would drive others to a rendezvous once I had checked by phone to Jay and Jill's house the next morning. As it turned out, by the time I had left nothing had happened but it was a good idea, and we can try again. The convoy comes down south every few weeks.

We had another musical evening. In fact, it was a pretty musical week. Jane has her cello, Ruth the tin whistle, Susan her mandolin and Angie her violin. Actually, Maureen and I feel rather out of things, as we agreed that we are the most unmusical people we know, but the musicians all agreed that they had to have an audience, so they would not throw us out of Orange camp. Dee told the story of Hansel and Gretel and we all made the right sound effect noises. Susan sang a blues version of Goldilocks and the three bears, we had a load of Irish and Welsh songs, and then we all drifted off to bed. Maureen said she would do night watch and I said she could wake me early and I would take over. It had been raining slightly all evening, but by this time it had cleared, so I went to bed again, near the fire in the Gore-Tex. However, it started again sometime in the night and I so wasn't all that worried when Maureen woke me at about 5.45, so I sat by the fire and made coffee and had a read. Dee got up and decided to walk to Blue, and then one by one, the others all drifted over to the fire. We had been rather short of wood, but as usual, we were provided with more, just when we needed it. Visitors keep us supplied and we have some large logs given by Newbury Council. Mind you, they do not know they provide them, but there are loads of work-experience youngsters around, picking up litter and putting posts in the ground to stop cars being driven or parked near us. To save them work, and to help us, they bring us posts for the fire. They are excellent and burn nice and slowly for ages. In return, we give them cups of tea, and when it rains, instead of getting soaked picking up litter, they take some from our pile and shelter with us. It is a very good arrangement. Someone gave us a few sacks of wood shavings and these are marvellous for getting the fire started when there is just a pile of ash. It has been too hot to have much of a fire going all the time, but we still need hot drinks and food.

We had many long discussion about the convoy, and what we are going to try and do next time is to blockade its return from inside rather than outside the base. This idea of 'cat flaps' makes sense and quite a lot will be made, fairly near gates and also quite close to the areas where the inner barbed wire rolls can be pulled back for patrolling purposes. This means that the cuts should not show too much, and anyway it will only be fence and wire close by, that are cut. As soon as the convoy is brought out, (we will obviously try to stop that happening as well), women will go inside the base and stay all night near Yellow, Orange, Blue and Indigo, which are the only gates that vehicles use. The women will be prepared with paint bombs, etc., and attack from inside, rather than outside the base. We think it should work well. I have asked that as soon as the convoy does comes out, that I want to be told, and will come to Greenham instantly.

On Tuesday morning Maureen, Susan, Penni and her Welsh friends all left, so Ruth, Jane, Julie, Angie and Lorraine who has come back to live with us, and I were left. Ruth and Lorraine went for a water run, when Jill from Red turned up and said they were being evicted. We rushed round to get everything organised, Jill went to find the brown van, and I put a load of stuff in my car, mainly the important items, like the cello, violin, and pickaxe and spade, the Brick Lane chair and personal possessions. Ruth and Lorraine came back, having dropped off the full water containers down the road, and we loaded food and almost everything in. We saw the red muncher at the end of the road, where it stopped to pick up the bags of rubbish collected by our work-experience friends. Then *blow me down*, if the muncher did not turn round and go back along the north side again. We had evicted ourselves for no reason! Actually, we were very glad that they had not come, as we now have a lot of mini benders round the place, both in the rabbit meadow and near the fire. During the rest of the day, we were finding our stock of wood, which we had chucked in the gorse and unloading the van as hunger overcame us. We had (well, the non-vegans) fresh herb scrambled eggs and *souped-up* tinned soup, then Angie and Julie decided to leaflet the American houses just outside the base near Blue. I said I would take them, as they had a lot of walking to do, as that night they wanted to leaflet the American houses inside the base.

The camps along the north side were very empty of possessions as the women were not sure that the muncher would not be back later that day, and I stopped on my way home at Red to find out if the bailiffs had evicted their secret bender near their garden. I talked to the real Jenny Williams for a while then came back to Orange. Suddenly there was a shout from the gate and four women from Emerald came and joined us. They had been inside the base, leaving visiting cards under windscreen wipers and inside cars. They had got into the base near the silos, having previously made their cat flaps, so just had to cut the inner wire. This had been done while visiting women from Blue had created a diversion and lots of noise. The break-in during broad daylight and so close to the silos was really great, and they had not been detained for more than 15 minutes after they got inside.

After the four women had eaten and had a coffee, Angie and Julie arrived back. They had been detained by the Americans, who had called the police. Then, they had been taken inside the base for questioning. They told the Emerald women that they wanted to go in the base that night, and they said they would support them and cut. A visitor who had just arrived said she would take them to Newbury to get more leaflets photocopied, as there were only a few left.

Margaret came back, so Ruth and Jane decided to get a lift from me to London and on our way, we dropped off the Emerald women. Margaret and Anne Francis have had a hard time with their Crown Court case. Anne is in prison, but Margaret was let off on a suspended good behaviour sentence for four months. They had a very hard time during the trial, as they were kept in Holloway and had to drive to Reading court every day, when they were either in court or in the cells. I do admire their strength; I do not think I could do it. One evening we had a talk about prison experiences, particularly about the ordinary women who were there. It really is another world, and those who had been inside all felt that prison was not the right place for many of the women who turn up there, particularly those with visa problems.

Driving Greenham women to London is always an amusing experience. Jane spent a lot of time trying to wipe off some of the dirty peanut butter, which was sticking to her face, then had a dry teeth cleaning session with the brush tied round her neck. Ruth during the journey was putting socks and shoes on her filthy feet, and they both maintained strongly that London was only a suburb of Greenham. I think I agree with them, but I did find a bath most essential in this large suburb before I did anything else.

30th August – 2nd September

Having had a few peaceful days in Wales, Orange Gate was reality this time. I could no longer park my car in the usual place, as the council had completed the circuit of posts. All vehicles are now on the road leading to the rabbit meadow. Reading Anne and Sally, Ruth and Jane, Susie, Johanna and Pattie, were all having breakfast/lunch, and they warmly greeted me. There was a long discussion about lending the brown van to Yellow, to take Verity and other women to Tepee Valley in Wales for a few days. We had been evicted that morning and one of the problems about lending the van is that we keep so much gear in it. It is quite essential at eviction time and, apart from that, it belongs to Marjorie, a Quaker, and we are responsible for it. Yellow women are not renowned for their care of vehicles, but Verity is ill and does need a change and help. Anyway, it was left that they could borrow it as long as we had a replacement big enough to load all out stuff into, and enough time to do this. I told the women my wedding ring story, and how Ellie, Clare and I had been to the Pig Shit festival a couple of weeks before. They told me about the Welsh Camp, swimming with a dolphin, and the arrests for walking along a road! I showed Anne the Alternative Energy leaflet, as she is hoping to go there soon and work there for a couple of months after Sally goes back to America in October. We also discussed the 10 Million Women for Ten Days event, and what would have to be done in the way of shit pits and an extra water supply. Everyone is quite convinced that a great many women will turn up and the whole thing will be a huge success, but there will be to be many problems. Apart from Sally going home, Ruth and Miranda are also returning to Australia and New Zealand. Orange Gate will not be the same without them, but other women will come and live instead.

After a while, and a few cups of coffee, Anne and I did a water run round to Yellow, and talked to Rebecca Johnson and Jane Dennet and some others. Anne assured me that I was the only woman she ever got soaked with on the water run, but I do not think this is fair as she was the one to splash us both. We then did a circuit, as our pickaxe had been lent to either Blue or Red. Blue Gate camp is quite different now. The council have put piles of earth on the usual site, so the women put wooden crosses on each mound, and moved themselves back into the woods in a much nicer place. They have a fantastic mobile kitchen on wheels, and the odd bender as well as tents. They look very comfortable, but did not have our pick, which was urgently needed, for another shit pit. We went on Red and they said that they had borrowed the pick, but unfortunately, during their eviction, one of the women had hidden it in a safe place, but she had now gone on holiday, and they could not find it! They lent us another tool, and then showed us their new bathroom, which was really impressive. Gateism is getting stronger, or perhaps it should be called *one-up-womanship*! On our way back, we got a couple of bottles of beer and then had supper, which was quite up to standard, in fact very good indeed. It is getting dark earlier these days, and we were sitting round the fire, when the familiar roar of a sports car sounded. Jill and Jay back from holiday in France. I was not surprised to hear that Jill had only managed one week in Peru, and jumped on a place and come home. She and Jay had gone to France for a week, but then stayed three. It was good to see them back again. The night watch from Abingdon arrived, so we were all able to go to bed. This is as essential for the vigilantes as for the convoy coming out, as in the past few nights, they had taken pot shots with an air rifle, slashed a tent, which luckily was not occupied, burnt and torn books, chucked stoned etc. I slept quite soundly in a very makeshift shelter near the old campfire place by Sally and Anne, having consumed my share of French plonk provided by Jill and Jay after the beer, and the disturbed previous night when I had been walked over and peed on by a kitten.

We moved the fire and kitchen to the other side of the shit pit lane as we felt it was slightly more sheltered. We could see Orange Gate more clearly from there. I do not think it will be so good in the rain, but it is not so windy here and the slight change of scenery is good. The kitchen tucks in nicely in the trees and the pram/washing up area is good. The next morning I got up and had a good wash, and decorated a tree with the knickers that I washed, then had a word with Anne and told her that we needed a slatted floor for the washing area, as feet -particularly when wet - pick up more dirt than one washes off. Well in no time at all, we made this amazing bathroom. A slatted floor, towel rail, clothes hooks a low table (which has been given as firewood the day before). All that was missing was a top, which we made from a wide plank. We put all the soap, toothpaste, toothbrushes, shampoo, etc. on it, and on the ground the *'body bowl'*, a water container and *'shower'*, which is a watering can. I put an upturned bucket to sit on, and we even found a piece of mirror for the table as well. A most elegant bathroom. The only trouble was that we could not find the hammer to nail the slatted floor together although we looked in the oven of the van where it is usually kept, but the next day I found it in the pram. Where else would we keep a hammer?

Overall Friday was a very domestic day. I did a marathon washing up session in the morning, got the kitchen in good order, moved firewood nearer the new fire place, talked to visitors, picked up my book about half a dozen times, but never read more than a few words before I was interrupted or distracted by something that was going on. Ruth left that day, so I moved my sleeping bag into her shelter. Julie arrived and sometime during that day informed me quite seriously that I was three times her age. God, that really made me feel good! Jan and Leslie arrived from Kent during the evening, and five women, the Guildford night watch came. During the day, we had visitors from Horsham and others from Lewis. I had talked to the phone and heard from John that we had been burgled and that his computer and disc-drive had been taken, and his waterproof gear had been nicked from his top box on the moped. By the end of that night, my shaky faith in human (male) nature had worn a lot thinner.

Anne was quite convinced that something was going to happen that evening so went off to bed at about 8.30 and asked me to wake her at 11.30 as that is about the time the vigilantes are on the prowl. By 11pm she was back at the campfire with the night watch, so as there were six women round the fire, I felt it was quite safe to go off to bed. I could not get to sleep. Perhaps Anne had infected me with her fears. Sometime later, actually 12.30, I heard a noise, something hitting the ground quite sharply, then silence. I listened intently, but there was no sound of footsteps running away. A few second later, Anne and the Guildford women came running up to make sure the sleepers were ok. Then I heard Ann call *"Fire!"* and got out of my sleeping bag into my clothes. The fire was at the other end of shit pit lane, on a piece of common where I'd put my tent some months ago. We rushed for water, which was in containers in the van where Anne and I had put it yesterday. I grabbed one, and ran (well, towards the end, staggered) towards the fire. A large area of common was ablaze, with sparks leaping across the paths. Luckily, the wind had died down, otherwise the damage would have been much worse. We tried to put water on it, and then discovered that another, quite separate fire, had been started further away, and so we put some

140

water on that. A woman asked the soldiers at the gate to call the fire brigade and police, and the police came quickly, although the fire brigade took ages. When they did arrive, were delayed further by the wooden posts blocking all paths round the edge of the common.

The police inspector was very concerned about the fire and about the vigilantes in general. He asked us to take note of car numbers with prowling male occupants, and said that he had had a couple of plain-clothes men watching the area for a few nights, but was too short staffed to patrol all the time. By this time, the fire had almost died down, and the firemen were beating out the last of the smouldering patches. We were all very depressed by the fire, but the next morning we realised that it had only burnt across all the tinder dry gorse and bracken, and had not done nearly as much damage as we thought. In fact, someone had stashed a bundle of firewood some time previously and it was still there, barely scorched, and with everything blackened round it.

We went back to our beds, but I did not sleep much. I think I heard every leaf in a square mile rustling, and was glad to get up early in the morning.

It was the first Saturday in the month, when we really get an influx of visitors. Anne had been telling us about a design she had seen for an oven, and all she needed were two oil drums. Well, Jane had seen one not far away, so we went and fetched it back to the camp. Rolling it back along the road was the most fun part of the exercise. The instructions as to its use were, *'first remove one end'*. Easier said than done, these things always are. Eventually we managed, although we did not have a big variety of tools. Most of them were various sized bolt cutters, and the largest worked at the cutting with a pipe wrench and hammer to pull back the metal and then have another go with the cutters. When we had finished we shoved the drum in the ditch, and put the burning paper in it to get rid of the kerosene dregs and smell. Anne thought that a dustbin for the inner part of the oven would be much easier than a second oil drum. I am sure she is right.

While this noisy work was going on our visitors were arriving. First, about a dozen a minibus from the South London Women's Hospital sit-in. They were great. Full of stories about the happenings there, the ineffectual security guards and authority in general. They have a real battle on their hands, but I am sure they are strong enough to succeed. They produced food and a box of wine, which they shared with us. I am certain we will meet again, and I promised to stay at the hospital sometime soon. We did have an idea for an exchange visit of hospital and Greenham women. We could go there and have hot baths (there are 47 in the hospital) and they could have a few days in the country.

After they left, we had a few minutes quiet then a brightly coloured bus arrived from London. A vast number of women piled out, and rather foolishly, I asked if anyone would like a cup of tea or coffee. They all did. It felt rather like the beginning of the ten million women, but they were lovely, supportive and friendly. When they were about to go, a woman in a wheelchair give me a pound to go towards some drink for that evening, I was really touched. Then Eileen turned up. She wanted a lift to Blue to do with communication and I took her round there, then on back to her house. We talked for ages, and she said that I could put my car in her field during the ten days if I wanted to, as I am scared of something happening to it. It does sound selfish, I know, but it is my freedom and independence.

By this time, Liz had turned up and Jane's sister Tammy. Jay was still hovering round, wondering how Jill had got on at home. We went to phone, but Jill was on her way back, and all seemed to be OK. A meal was prepared by Liz, which was good. Then we all felt we needed a drink, so four or us went off to Thatcham where we arrived at the Off Licence 2 minutes after it closed, so rushed to Newbury, then back to the camp. We sat and talked and some of the women sang. It was one of those really good Orange Gate evenings. No one wants to leave the fire and go to bed. It is good to sit there with good company on a warm summer night round a campfire, with a drink. The night watch was shared out, and I stayed up until about 1.30. I did feel that we might have vigilante trouble again that night, but I was not disturbed, and slept soundly. I got up at about 9 o'clock, went to get my washing things from the car, and looked at the brown van. Something odd about it. Sally was near me and I asked her when the back window had been broken and we realised it had been done during the night. There was a hole in it the size of a first, and the rest of the glass was completely crazed. We told the others and were discussing what time it happened, when a Red Gate woman came along. She said that she knew that the glass had been broken before us, from the soldiers on watch at her gate. It appears that one of the guards at our gate had seen a man do it! The guard

142

had been talking to a couple of the women for ages and had never mentioned it to them. Apparently, the incident took place when we were all awake, in the evening. I cannot be bothered to talk to the solders, there are not many of them around anyway, and when I hear of things like this, I realise it's a complete waste of time trying to communicate with them. We will tell the police of course, and let them get information from the guard.

Before I left, I had a good wash in the bathroom and changed into clean clothes for London. I hope the bathroom is not evicted, but it is well back from the fire area, so should be all right. Sally and Anne were going a little later as Anne had to be in court in Wales for Tuesday. We all had a late breakfast of scrambled eggs and toast. We will all meet again soon. I plan to be back at Orange Gate on the 18th September, which is in just over two weeks' time, ready for 10 million women.

One amusing thing happened on Saturday. I was talking to Jane Dennett, and discovered that her first job on coming to Greenham was to clean out Peter Darlington van ready for Norman and me to collect. She agreed with me about the filth and chaos, and said she was amazed I had come back again, and I said I was amazed she had stayed!

19th September 1984

I have only been here 24 hours, but thought I would start writing now while I have a bit of space. The first day was great as so many women I have not seen for a long time where either already here or arrived during the day. Sally, (Anne was away for the day on a course), Joanna, Annie, Rebekah, American Liz, Miranda, Margaret, Jane, Jay, Jill; Sian and Kay for a little while, women from Red Gate, which had been evicted so many times, they abandoned it, but have now set it up again.

To begin at the beginning. My car was loaded up with goods from Deal. Bill gave me a sack of potatoes, three boxes of tomatoes, onions, carrots, sweet corn, etc., plus two huge homemade loaves from Claudine. What with the tents, my usual gear, plus stuff from Hilary, I was very laden. During the day, I put my tent up behind the shit pit area next to American Liz's new bender, did a load of washing up, and handed out quantities of potatoes and tomatoes to women who came round from other gates. I met some new residents like Ann and her three daughters from Burton, and Pauline and her friend who arrived from Holland and Chris from Cumbria. Later on, I cooked potatoes and all the sweet corn for supper. Most of the day was taken up with talking and exchanging news. Most of us feel rather apprehensive about the next few days and whether it will work out, but we will have to just wait and see.

Greenham seems to be suffering from a flea crisis, but so far, I have not been bitten. Last night, I moved my sleeping bag into Liz's amazing new bender, *The Elephant*, rather than sleeping in my tent. It is very long and comfortable, and it is good to lie back and see the branches with leaves still on just over my head. The benders are creeping back in out-of-the-way places, and I think before long there will be lots of them, all tucked away out of sight. The most ingenious is Juley's. She spent a couple of days digging a deep pit and then put a low construction over the top of polythene, then branches over that for disguise. The evictions have been very bad recently, but yesterday we were expecting to have another one, and today we are just waiting. The traveller, Sally, was told by the police that we were all going to be finally evicted today, but I think it is just bluff. Just to be on the safe side we have put most of the food etc. in the brown van so the rest can be quickly picked up and pushed away in the pram, or carried off.

Tommy and Danny are back with their parents, and they have not changed much. Four of us were sitting in my car having a drink and a talk, when we saw them creep into the van and take something out. They had nicked our candles and lit then down the road. We went and got them back, but we will have to be careful to keep everything locked up while they are around.

Liz gave us a 'film show' last night. We were sitting in the car and she said she thought we looked like a drive-in movie, so got out and gave us this amazing drama with lots of characters, either with or without a hat. It was about Peter Fonda and, I think, Jesus. It was confusing, but funny. Rebekah, Jane and I fell about laughing, even more so when the motorbike fell over. It was not actually part of the act, and luckily, no damage was done. Later Liz and I said we would do some of night watch as no one turned up for it. In the end, the other two stayed up with us around the fire until about 1.30 and we stayed up very sleepily until 2.30 then went to bed.

This morning is quiet. We are all feeling a little apprehensive about what will happen. The influx has not yet arrived.

20th & 21st September 1984

I am sitting in the car surrounded by activity. Maybe there are not 10 million, but there are an awful lot of women around and I am having a break from making a shit pit shelter, remaking the bathroom, which the bailiffs destroyed, and general cooking, talking and sharing activities.

Yesterday the women started to arrive, a steady stream of them. Most seem to be self-sufficient, some of the regulars are bringing food and goods with them to the main fire, and now there are dozens of little camps all around Orange Gate. In one direction, they stretch pretty well back to the main road, and the other way they are filling the rabbit meadow, the clearing, and odd tents are scattered back on to the common wherever there is a clear bit of ground. There are lots of fires and cooking activities, all of which are observed frequently by the police helicopter, which hovers overhead in its usual irritating and noisy fashion. Work goes on inside the base, where they are digging a huge pit just inside the gate. We hoped for a while they were going to make a tunnel just so we could get in the base easier, but I do not think this is the intention.

It is becoming impossible to name all the women whom I know that have arrived, but Diana and her mother and daughter came yesterday, Judy, Jan, Di and a huge crowd from Southampton, Abergavenny women, Joyce and by the end of the day only Cleis and Toni-the-potter had not seen.

I really ought to go back to where I left off the day before yesterday. As I mentioned we were all wondering what would happen, and the day rather drifted about in a non-particularly constructive fashion. We felt we ought to make things and prepare, but the time was not right. Eventually Faversham Hilary arrived and we put up her big tent next to mine. It was not that easy as the brambles and trees rather got in the way. However, we now have this little private enclave, sheltered and quiet. Jay is building herself and Jill an underground shelter nearby, but apart from them, there is no one else around. We had just about finished, and were wondering whether to go off to the pub, when Mike drove up with Hil and Liz. We set up the gear in the tents and then wandered over to the fire where Rebekah was cooking a great meal. There was a fair amount of drink round so we all sat and talked then Liz did another film show on Humphrey Bogart, the East German supplies of bolt cutters, and the pusher of them (who was a little old woman from Birmingham!) It was highly complex and very funny.

Somehow, we did not get to bed all that early again. Hil and I had a nightcap with Hilary and Liz in their tent, and then I really crashed out and slept very soundly apart from waking to hear heavy rain falling. It went on all night and quite a lot of the day. By the middle of the morning the puddles were really deep, so we dug drainage trenches into the massive shit pit, and it is not too bad now. The police are here in some force, plus a couple of mounted men, and they walk round all the time, and have at least one van parked at the gate, making sure we behave ourselves. We are wondering what sort of action will take place. We would love to have something really peaceful and quiet where the fence just disappears and falls down of its own accord, with no loud pulling and cutting and shouting violence and tension. We will have to think hard and constructively, and even then, I don't see how we can achieve this, but at Greenham anything is possible.

I had arranged with Jay that I would help her collect her caravan from north of Banbury with Jill, when she finished school. In the end, Hil and Juley also came with us. I had no idea it was going to be such a long trek, and I drove over 160 miles on this jaunt. Actually, it was fun. We saw some lovely countryside, found some amazing mushrooms in the Quaker graveyard, and Jay now has a home of her own near Thatcham, in a nice paddock. Mind you, the caravan needs a lot of working on, and it is missing windows and is only a shell, but I know it will be successful. As she said, she could not stand a *Pommie winter under a sheet of plastic*! We did not get back to Orange Camp until well after 10pm, but we had stopped for chips in Thatcham, so we were not that hungry. We had a couple of beers and a snack, and then went off to bed. The tent is good just a bit wet round the zip, but it has always been bad there.

We do have one other real problem at Greenham, mainly Orange Gate. Fleas. We may not have 10 million women, but we do have 10 million fleas, and they are breeding rapidly. The first night in American Liz's bender, she told me the fleas were bad and showed me the bites all over her back. They did attack my right shin, but I am not flea material and Annie and I are not the only women in this area who are not constantly scratching somewhere about our persons. What interests me is what will happen when we all go home. Will the flea epidemic spread around the country, or will the

10 million badge be a woman scratching, or just the picture of a flea? Greenham fleas are everywhere, is a good slogan and most appropriate to this gathering.

Annie's Flea Song

The time for fleas is coming near,
Jump off the cats and in the beer.
10 million fleas bite wimmin here
10 million women fear.

Chorus

> *September 20th for 10 days*
> *Fleas come together to find new places,*
> *Judy's armpits, Liz's back,*
> *The fleas are on the attack.*

It's time to scratch, it's time to itch,
The fleas will land on every witch.
TCP cream makes them flinch,
But they bite on inch by inch.

Chorus

Stop the nukes and break the law
No multinationals anymore
Wimmin bring the government to their knees,
But they can't stop the fleas.

Chorus

Two fairies in pink tutus, leaping round waving wands and turning all the policemen into frogs have just interrupted me. The cops do not really realise this yet, but soon they will suffer an identity crisis.

Today we have, *got ourselves together*. The camp is full of women making things. Annie is painting notices. Hil, Hilary and Liz have dug a deep shit pit in the usual area and made a screen round it, as the police and various men keep walking up and down shit pit lane. The loo is now in position over the *council shit pit*, which is actually a long trench to stop us bringing cars on to the common. The construction consists of a floor with a hole, standing on strong supports, then four uprights and non-see-through plastic surround. It has to be strong and heavy as the wind is blowing like mad, and the floor has to take the heaviest women. When it was finished and we carried it down to the far end of the ditch, Ruth was persuaded to squat inside and have the inaugural pee. *Success!*

I have re-instated the bathroom. It may not be quite as good as the original structure. I had difficulty in finding the right sort of wood, and the slatted floor is nailed to the ground, as the only nails were 4 inches long. What made me want to put it in order again was that I had a '*bath*' this morning and it really is hard not to get dirty feet while washing.

I am having trouble (at the moment, as I write this) because Hil is distracting me in wonderment at my touch-typing. Anyway, now all is quiet. The sun is shining and women just wandering about, waiting for the real onslaught tomorrow. (I hope.)

24th September 1984

The rest of Friday is a bit of a blur. It is so hard to remember details of what happened, except the unimportant things, like the fact I missed supper again that evening. I have just remembered what did take place. Juley, Hil, Jan, Maureen and I decided that we would get supper at Green as they had said there was going to be a big gathering, rave-up and food there. Well we set off and it was very dark, with masses of cars and women all wandering around. There were many fires, but the food being cooked on them was obviously just for a few. Then we saw a big fire with women standing round and chanting and singing going on. We had found the right place (or so we thought). A bag of peanuts was passed round and we were told to take one each and pass the bag on. Then some dried fruit and the same thing happened. Then some cheese, then one piece of Ryvita, so we all broke off a small bit and passed it on. The trouble was that we passed all these things on to German women who did not understand that they had to pass it round, so it kept coming back to us, and we were so hungry that we gladly kept nibbling. Then a very small bottle of homemade beer reached us. This we did not even try to pass round, but stood and shared it amongst ourselves. Somehow, we did not seem to be really joining in the spirit of the occasion, and decided to creep away and go to the pub. Well we ended up having a good evening there, and it was only later that we found we had left Green much too early, had missed the proper food. We had also missing the pulling down of the Green Gate gate, and a load of fencing. You cannot win them all, but we really failed badly that evening. The odd thing was that *all* the Orange Gate women had done the same thing, and gone away much too early.

Back at Orange, we sat around. Then Reading Anne said that she had heard that bits of the Cruise convoy were going to be brought back inside that night. She even had a time for this exercise, 3.30am but this rumour was one that I was not very keen on. Anne, Hil and St. Albans Anne said that they would go and lurk in a car on the appropriate road, and I said I would direct operations from this end, from my bed. By the time we had all this worked out it was 1.30am. When Hil crawled back into the tent at 4am she woke me briefly to say nothing had happened, I felt I had taken the right decision. She agreed.

The twelve women from Deal also arrived safely on Friday night at about midnight. We went and talked to them and watched them put up a couple of tents, and helped them drink their apricot brandy.

Saturday was a day of greeting more women and showing them where everything was, and saying that they should put their tents wherever they could find an agreeable space. That was not easy as the tents and vehicles stretch from the road right round to the clearing, which is full, as well as the rabbit meadow, and on to the common. Moira and waffle- woman-Jan are here, plus a load more I know from all over the country. The weather is quite good, sunny, but the wind typically Greenham, blowing smoke from the fire in all directions.

Ellie turned up during the afternoon, and we decided to have fish and chips, and to take Jan, Rebekah and Maureen to the Rockaby for a drink. There was to be an action to be held at Orange that night at 8pm, mainly singing and then a silent period. Actually, we were rather late back for it, and found the road quite blocked with women and police. So, backed the car down the road and, on Rebekah's advice, went round the back and took a *very* narrow track up to the main path... but found it blocked by a tent. Therefore, I had to back-down it again, and reach home via shit pit lane.

Some women were pulling the fence and the police kept hauling them back, but there were no arrests and the whole thing was low key. At this time, the only women arrested from Orange were Miranda and Reading Anne. They had found a newly blown down piece of tree, which they wanted to use to make a bender pole. The police saw them and accused them of damaging the common, so they have been charged. They were both upset as they are both very caring as far as the common is concerned and are women who do not cut trees down.

We all had a drink of mulled wine round the fire then Ellie and I had a walk down to the ford before going to bed, where Ellie lost her lighter in the ford under the bridge. These stupid things do happen. Sally's parents arrived today from America and Barbara was just as enthusiastic about the camp as the last time I saw her.

Sunday did not really start until midday when we got up and had breakfast. Women were milling around in their thousands, so Ellie and I decided to walk round the base. We stopped at Red and walked on past Violet and Indigo. Blue was packed as they had been doing a blockade and an All Women's Band from Nottingham was playing. We felt it was time for a rest, so had some coffee under the shelter when the rain suddenly poured down. The ground was really wet in places, but we went straight past Turquoise and Emerald round to Green. We took one look at the muddy boots of the women heading towards us, and took the longer way round by road. I saw many more women I knew on the walk, including some of the miners' wives from East Kent.

At Yellow, we sat by the fire and Caroline Blackwood turned up. She handed over a bottle of vodka, and then said who she was. She listened carefully to criticism, and said would correct them in her next book. I thought it was brave of her to come and be prepared to listen to the complaints anyway, and was glad that most of the women thought her book was really good.

We saw Juley at Yellow. She had been in a blockade, and had been dropped on her head. She looked rather shaky, so Barbara got her a lift back home, and Ellie and I walked. I also saw Jane and met her mother who is staying at Yellow.

Ellie got a lift back to London with Isia soon after we got back, so I wandered down to talk to the Deal women who, of course, had just gone, apart from Andrea who is staying on. I stopped and chatted to the St. Albans crowd and was invited to a superb curry supper with hot cooked fruit for pudding. It was really welcome. Back at the main fire we felt that there should be some action that night. In the end, there were quite a lot of us prepared to do it, so we ended up with two groups. These split down into smaller groups, and none of us had any luck. The first lot went towards Yellow, round the corner from here, and there were lurking men both inside and outside the fence, creeping around, and hiding in bushes pretending not to be there even when the women confronted them. Karen and Fiona from the London Hospital went round the other way, and as Karen was bending down for the first snip, lights were shone on her with bolt cutters poised, so she beat a hasty retreat. Then Faversham Hilary and I wondered if we could find the hole, which (we hoped) the first group had cut. So, we strolled round, but we were spotted instantly by an MoD cop and his dog. They were both very quiet, but we backed away into the bushes, and in a few moments met up with the women also on their way back. We are not very happy about things. Either the MoD has got really clever and is playing our game of hide-and-seek, or else we have a mole at Orange. I really hope it is the first, but I am not at all sure.

I went to bed early last night, and really slept soundly, but I knew there was going to be a blockade at Orange at 7, so was not all that surprised to be woken by Reading Anne just before. Hil was not at all keen to get out of her sleeping bag, but we staggered over to the gate and sat in front of it, in varying degrees of sleepiness and alertness. There were a lot of us there, and we decided it was important to go to Indigo to blockade there, as the gate is being used all the time.

I never managed to *even start* writing about my real event of the 24th, as the interruptions just went on and on, but now I have some space. Juley has joined me in the car with knitting, orange juice and a streaming cold. All is quiet.

The blockade at Orange was going pretty well, but we felt that we had so many women around a crowd of us ought to go to Indigo, which is very much in use, the police are being very heavy and there are not too many women there. Some of us piled into the brown van and set off. Women from all gates were there, milling about and we were told that they had been warned that if they obstructed the road again, they would be arrested. Well, we decided that we had not been warned, so Steph and I from Orange and Mersey Karen and five others, from Blue I think, went into the road and prepared to sit down. Well, my bottom never reached the ground before two very large policemen grabbed me under the armpits and carried me away. I must be fair and say that they were careful not to hurt me and when one of them lost his grip, the other stopped and told him exactly how to hold me. Karen and others were dragged quite roughly, and her shoe was wrenched off. Anyway, for the first time I ended up in the golf club car park. I was asked if I would get into the van on my own, or would I rather be dragged. I decided that I preferred to go in under my own steam, and soon the eight of us were locked in and being driven to Newbury cop shop.

When we arrived, we were processed one by one. I was taken in third. I had been warned that I may have my photo taken, and to hold a scarf over my head, but of course, I was taken by surprise when it happened. I do not think it was much of a picture, as I had my hand up to my face, as usual dragging on a cigarette. A policeman took me to a cell, where I was asked to empty my pockets. I had the usual odds & ends of rubbish in them, and money in my sock. Even my watch was taken and put in the bag with everything else, tobacco, lighter, rusty nail, gloves, coffee bag etc. I was then taken to the charging officer who asked my name, "Janette Leech", date of birth, I can't remember the date I gave except that I've decided that each time I'm arrested I will get a year younger, and place of birth, "Chalfont St Peter", again. I think it sound very authentic. I told the officer that I had not been warned that I would be arrested if I went into the road, and actually, no one had arrested me yet. He said he was doing so now. They accepted my address as the Peace Camp, and he asked me if I would like to make one phone call. As the time was about 8am I did wonder if I ought to make a call to John to tell him it was time to wake up and go to work, but it in the end, thought it would not be diplomatic. Anyway, after signing a couple of bits of paper, I was taken to my cell and locked in.

For the uninitiated, I must say it was a very boring place, just like the ones you see on the telly. The walls had been newly painted and I was warned that if I damaged them in any way, I would be fined. Mind you, anything that I could have used to scratched marks on the walls had been removed, but my shoes had not been taken as they fasten with Velcro rather than laces.

Shortly after the door had clanged shut, it was unlocked and a policewoman asked me if I would like some tea. I said no I would rather have coffee. "With or without sugar?" "Without, thank you." A few moments later, she returned with the coffee, and said she would put it on the bench for me as the plastic cup very hot. She then asked me if I wanted breakfast, and did I eat meat? I said yes to both questions and she asked if sausages would be all right. Once again, I said yes. Door clanged shut. A while later she brought in a *huge* plateful of food; two sausages, half a tin of baked beans, a fried egg and two tomatoes! Amazing! I really enjoyed my meal. When the empty plate was taken away, she said she would get me another coffee. When she brought this a while later, she said it was hard to remember, but she hoped that it was correct without sugar.

When I told the women about this back at Orange, they could hardly believe it, as they only had cups of lukewarm tea, they felt they were lucky. Most women are all keen on organising another pre-breakfast action to see if they get a similar meal. The policewoman was really nice.

My cell was right at the end of the passage, but I could hear women from our group singing in the distance and we tried to have an '*I Spy*' game, and percussion sessions on the grills under the wooden bed/seat. It was bloody cold in my cell, and I curled up on the bench and dozed for a while. It is very hard to know how much time has passed, and even a short while seems hard to bear with absolutely nothing to do, except live with your own thoughts. In my cell, I had a block of those thick glass wall panels, which let in a bit of light, and I found myself counting them. Nine across and five down. Forty-five in all. Just to check I counted them individually! I did not feel particularly claustrophobic; I just wondered how long they would keep me in. I guessed how much time passed, and when I was released, I was interested to find it was about an hour later than I thought it would be: 11.30 rather than 10.30. When they started to let us go, the first woman shouted back, that she was going out and we would all be free soon. The actual release meant that our possessions were taken from the sealed bag and checked with us, and then the charge sheet was handed over. I have to appear in the magistrates' court on the 5th November. That is a Monday so we will all have a big party over the weekend, and I will take an *exeat* from University. So many women have already been arrested; they will never get through all the cases on that day.

There were masses of women waiting on the steps for us outside, and we stopped on the way home to buy a bottle of scotch to go with our morning coffee. We stopped to drop someone at Red, and they told me that a Rounders game had been arranged between Red and Orange for that afternoon after the blockade at Indigo. They wanted to play where the Americans play football, on the end of the runway. The plan was to cut the fence, then the two teams to go in, with bat and ball.

We had coffee and lunch, then I sat in the car to write, but after a bit, urgent lifts were needed, so I started being a taxi, first for the blockade, then an hour later to pick them up. Our team was depleted a bit as Jan and Helen had been arrested. I think Hil and Liz and Hilary were quite disappointed not to be arrested as well, but they were looking forward to the game. Juley borrowed my cutters for the hole, and Maureen got into the spirit of the Rounders by taking off her jacket and putting running shoes on. However, once again, the MoD were there, ready and waiting. I had decided not to take part, as I thought two arrests in one day was pushing my luck too far. In the end, the women went off in dribs and drabs round towards Red where Juley had previously cut a hole which no one had found. They all got inside, were spotted by the police and I think it was more a game of tag rather than Rounders.

Everyone was impressed by Maureen's running speed, and at one point she was in danger in lapping the man chasing her! They were eventually rounded up and questioned in the base. They were not charged, and were lucky enough to be released at Orange.

I went back to Red with some women and then on to Newbury to get petrol and make phone calls. I called round to the police station and saw Jan and Helen standing on the steps, waiting for the other to be released and their lift to collect them. We had a drink then Sheriden came in her Dormobile and we all drove home. We had a meal, and as I was tired, decided to go to bed early. I went and cleaned my teeth (I had not even washed my hands or face all day) then there was the suggestion of hot chocolate and brandy, so stayed up for hours talking round the fire. I never even heard Hil come to the tent, a short while after I gone to bed.

25th, – 27th September 1984

The 25th was another day of arrivals and departures. Lynne and Susan came from Wales, Waffle Jan is going to live in France with her fellow, and Annie has decided that she will go grape picking with them for a while. We decided we would have a party for Jan that night and mulled wine was on the menu. There were a lot of strange women round the campfire, so one by one we wandered off to Diana's fire, and were checking the wine was the right flavour, until unfortunately we found we had finished it before Jan and Moira appeared. They did have a bottle of scotch with them, so it was not as disastrous as it might have been, and everything ended with a load of songs by Moira, Jan and Annie mostly. By this time, I was speechless with laryngitis again, so all I could manage was a rather bad clapping rhythm noise. I must try hard not to talk too much.

Earlier on in the evening we were told that two South African women were giving a show round at Green Gate called Wenzani (*"What are you doing?"*) in which she asks questions rather than gives answers. A crowd of us went to see them, and they were fantastic. They gave a series of sketches of life in South Africa, most of them sad and very moving, some funny, and they sang the songs of the black people. By the time they finished it was quite dark, so they borrowed a torch from a member of the audience and continued by the light from it. We were all very moved and felt close to them, but realised that our lives were easy in comparison with the brutality of the police and hatred of the whites.

We are still feeling very neurotic about the actions, which appear to be known about inside the base before we even start them. I am still not sure whether this is because at last the authorities are getting cleverer and more cunning, or whether there is a *'mole'*. We all feel that proposed actions are discussed too freely, and it is more than likely that there are any *'plants'* amongst us, so now we have little huddles and try to keep actions fairly secret. I thought it was just Orange that was feeling like this, but I find it is all the gates, and that Yellow are in even more of a state than we are.

Anyway, after this Waffle Jan party, I was feeling merry, and just about to go to bed when Barbara from Yellow turned up looking for Juley. I had only been to Juley's underground bender once in daylight, and trying to find it in the dark was more than I could cope with. I came back and found Gravesend Jan, who was in a worse state than I was, but knew how to find the bender. We set off hand in hand, crashing through the undergrowth, and woke Juley from a deep sleep (it was well past midnight), told her Barbara wanted to see her, and went back to camp. Barbara had left by this time, but Juley was very good about it, and not *too* cross with us for waking her. I would have been furious if anyone had done that to me, whatever the circumstances.

The next morning I was up by 8am and took Juley to Yellow, before driving to Worthing to see my mother. It was a good day to be away, as it gave me a chance to save my non-existent voice, have a bath and do a load of washing. I got back just before 7pm, in time for a good supper and a sit round the fire. I was thinking about going to bed at 10.30, but was not particularly tired, when two women, one from Yellow and one from Orange wanted a lift round to Red. I realised there was action in the air, so offered my services as a driver. It turned out to be quite a long night. Burghfield was the objective. A woman from Red joined us and we set off. I really felt I was the *'get-away'* driver, but I am not sure if a Fiat Panda is quite the right vehicle. We had lots of complicated maps to find the back way round so we would not be seen, and I pulled the car just off the road and they piled out with the usual equipment of cutters and paint.

We arranged that I would wait for 2 hours in the car, and if they had not returned by then I would go. I dozed for a while, and only four vehicles passed during the next hour and a half. Then I heard running. The three had been spotted. They had cut a hole, having gone across a field, scrambled through brambles etc. When they were at the fence, they had seen nothing but one of them had heard the click of a bike gear or dynamo, although no light was seen. Then they heard a policeman on a walkie-talkie say that *"two peace women were around"*, so the three of them fled.

The action was useful for future occasions of how to be more successful. I said that the driver needed more instruction, such as the names that were to be given if they were arrested, and now long to leave before checking where the women were. In addition, if they needed much longer than two hours, the car needed to be parked safely, and arrangements had to be made for the cutters to get back to Juley and me.

As usual, the cutting sounded incredibly loud, but at last it was done, and just as the women round us were about to go, I saw five women *behind* us creeping towards the fence... *a rival group from Yellow!* I leapt up and told them that Orange women were going in *now*, and if they would like to wait a bit, they could use the same hole. I warned them not to go near the hangers, which were where our group was heading. They thanked us for providing the hole, and then they crawled through. Juley, their woman with the cutters and I walked back in the rain to Yellow. Marie and Io gave us a lift back home and hospital Karen produced the wine. Isia turned up, and so another evening started. I was so tired that I could not stay up all that long, but I was still around when women were let out of Orange Gate. They had gone quite a long way inside before being caught, and had not been charged. They had had the usual fun and games in the prefab where they were taken for interrogation, and as usual, I think the cops were only too glad to be rid of them.

Big Liz's car has been decorated. Apart from a huge web and a witch on a broomstick and a poem, Orange women have been doing self-portraits, in characteristic poses. I did myself standing on my head with a bottle beside me!

This morning I have been sitting here next to the car while Penni drew a lovely picture of Sian with Tim lying on her stomach, then one of me typing. The police are everywhere and the Royal Irish Rangers are back in action inside the base. The sun is shining, and women are everywhere, more and more. The police have been trying to count us, and apart from their choppers, an army one is now overhead. They are all quite certain a big action will take place tomorrow, but we don't seem to have heard about it, on this side of the fence. Last night when Sheriden was inside the police kept asking her about actions, so she told them that the big action was going to happen at 6am this morning. I don't know whether they believed her.

We had a bit of fun with them this morning. St Albans Anne decided to put her tent up where the benders used to be along the fence, so a few of us went to help. The police waited until the tent was up, then came and asked us to take it down. I counted and there were 18 police lurking in our area. That is known as overkill. We kept them talking and arguing while we smoked our cigarettes, then they started pulling out the pegs and getting quite cross, so we took it away and put it up somewhere else.

Time for coffee and lunch now, I think.

29th & 30th September 1984

I am back home now and my interruptions are different. The phone, the cat and rushing in and out, having to deal with the washing on the line in a day of heavy showers. In my mind, I am still back at Orange and yesterday afternoon I returned a load of Hil's possessions to her and we sat and talked for hours. Like me, she cannot wait to get back there again. We were both pretty tired, but a bit of sleep gets rid of that. We cannot get rid of the memories and experiences nearly so easily.

I stayed round the main camp area and my car on Saturday until Christine and Ellie arrived. They were amazed at the number of women there, so I took them on a tour round to see the rest of the population round Orange. Then we had a coffee with free-food people, collected some things for them from their house, and decided that we would have an early drink at the Rockaby. Juley joined us, as she wanted to be dropped at Red Gate, but in the end stayed with us. The Rockaby so early in the evening was not its usual self and had more locals rather than Greenham women there, but gradually it became more normal. We did not stay late, as we knew that at 8 o'clock there was going to be a big gathering at Orange. This time I was sure I would not be able to drive down the road, so took the back way up shit pit lane. There were thousands of women around. When we first got there, they were just singing, and then they sat silently then hummed. There was a bit of a noise down the road, and soldiers inside forming up and moving to where the noise was so all the women cheered, and then moved in towards the fence. There was banging and yelling and feelings, and the mood changed. Anything might happen. I saw Reading Anne and Sally both looking very apprehensive as not only women could get hurt. There were children around, and dogs, and the tension was rising. The trouble is that women come to Greenham for a big demo and they want to do something. They are so used to the usual life style of being organised and told what to do that they look for leaders. The residents do not want hierarchy but neither do they want violence. The fence pulling gives a great feeling of power, and we all know that after only a few moments it rocks and is loose. However, the posts are heavy concrete, and there is barbed wire on the top of the fence. Pushed or pulled over, people can be badly hurt, and the police and soldiers are frightened and lash out indiscriminately. Cutting the wire with bolt cutters may take longer but it is not as dangerous.

I was not as scared as other residents about the feelings, I had. I had done a bit of banging myself on the big skip with a stone, but realised this banging made the tension worse, so stopped and stood quietly. Slowly the noise stopped and women came back from the fence a little, then starting singing Greenham songs again. We were relieved to hear them, and I told Sally I thought this would happen but the emotions would go in waves and the fence shaking would start again, and then die down. Anne said she felt it would be a good idea to try to disperse everyone by 9 o'clock, so went round and suggested it to various groups. I should say that all this took place just round the gate, but up and down the road, groups of women were *doing their own thing*, some cutting, some shaking and banging, but the main crowd were in agreement. At 9 o'clock, they drifted off to their tents and all was quiet.

Odd shots and songs round the fence went in for hours, but it was not so frenetic. I heard that there was going to be another big action at 4am, but when the time came, I was tucked up in my sleeping bag and the rain was beating down. I will have other opportunities to go inside the base, and I do not feel an action when the place is so crowded is right, for me.

We went back to the fire, had a drink and found to our amazement there was still some food in the wok, so shared it out. One of the women left her little boy Joseph with us, and I sat him between my legs where he played with a candle and a stick for over an hour quiet happily, having been rather scared at first. By about 10.30, we decided it was time for bed. The little tent next to mine has been empty all week, so Christine put her sleeping bag in there. Sometime during the night, I was aware of voices near my head and the owner of the tent, Mary, had come back. There was just room for the two of them, but they did get a bit wet, as a real storm had got up and it was with lashing rain. I couldn't be bothered to get up and fasten the piece of polythene I'd put over the door of my tent in place, but kept my feet well away from the entrance and we only had a small puddle inside by the morning, which didn't really worry us.

I got up quite early, about 9.30, as I wanted to make a couple of phone calls. Once again, the receiver had been ripped out of the local box and I went onto Brimpton. Making phone calls in that area has become a nightmare for us all. A few evenings previously, I had made the most expensive call of my life, which I did not want to do that again. The first phone box I tried was full of money, and would only make reverse charge calls. The second, just in Thatcham, was vandalised. The third swallowed 10p pieces then went dead. The fourth was occupied for ages. When eventually I got on the line, there was no reply. So I went to the off-licence, bought a bottle of scotch, took it back to Orange and it was drunk in about 5 minutes!

By the time I got back for breakfast, the coaches were arriving and by midday, we could hardly move. Donations were flooding in and we set up a big box of food for miners' wives and children. We are worried that the bailiffs will be very heavy this week, so it is no good keeping more than can be coped with during evictions. Some of the homemade food was fabulous. There was one two foot square chocolate cake given one day, just as the TV crew for CBS in America was about to have an interview with Sally and American Liz, so it will be shown to the American audience. At times, it is really to keep a straight face. Sometime on Sunday when every two minutes the residents were being asked some questions, a nice woman came up to me with a carrier bag. She explained she thought we might find the things she had brought would be useful, which they will be, then pulled out some cut pieces of string which she said could be tied round individual candles and hung from the women's waists during eviction time! I managed not to catch anyone's eye at this, but in some ways I wish she, and others, could see the mayhem with bailiffs striding round, pulling hidden items from the bushes, women pulling them back claiming them as personal property, the pram overflowing with pots, pans, dishes and cutlery, and the desperation and scurrying around. Tying candles onto belts is about the last thing we would have time to do, however brilliant an idea it might seem to someone who has obviously never experienced an eviction. A lot of money donated has been spent on essentials, like new tyres for the brown van, and giving women some dole money, which they have not had for weeks. I am not sure how much I took in cash and cheques during the ten days and kept in my locked car, but it was quite a few hundred pounds. We are so short of money, this really will help for a few weeks. Also, we had blankets, clothes and a tarpaulin, all of which are needed now the weather is getting colder. Benders in the bushes will need to be carefully hidden from prying eyes. Someone offered a tent, and I found Isia and told her, as hers has been one of those slashed by vigilantes some weeks ago. The replacement is identical to the destroyed one.

Orange Gate hairstyles are really good. Anne cut one or two others and mine early on in the week. Then Listy set about most of the heads around. Juley, we discover actually has ears, and Jan's long hair is now fashionably short on top, although still long round the side and back. Some have natural spikey hair and those with fine hair had gel put on the make it stick-up. The police will not recognise us next time they arrest us. We hope!

It has been very interesting how new affinity groups have organised themselves. Hil, Hilary, Liz, Sheridan, Jan. Helen, Maureen, Big Liz (and a few more) have formed a close group, and will meet up for more actions and companionship. I am more in tune with the original Orange Gate women, but we will not be the same soon as Ruth is going back to Australia any day now and, in a couple of weeks, Sally is going back to America, although I am certain she will be back perhaps next year. American Liz is also going back at Christmas, and Miranda in the New Year to New Zealand. We will really miss these strong women. I know that others will come and be strong, but we all came to Orange at more or less the same time and have a deep understanding and love for each other. Goodbyes are really sad with such good and true friends.

Perhaps for me one of the best things about ten day was meeting friends again. On Sunday, just for the day, Marion and Ann-the Vicar's wife came, plus Dot, Kay and others from Wales. Charmaine, Dot's daughter had had a strange experience a couple of days earlier when she was cutting the fence, was spotted, chased, then rugby tackled by a policeman, and then she got an asthma attack. The cop was really worried, got help, stayed with her in the ambulance and refused to have her arrested, just sat and held her hand, until he was sure she was all right. She said she thought the experience of this would make him a more thoughtful man.

During all this activity, Reading Anne and I were trying to continue our work on the oven. Anne had put the drums in place over the fire hole near the main fire behind the woodpile, and we then set about mixing cement and sealing it in position. At one point Anne went off to help start a car, and Val helped, then I did a bit on my own. When the cement is hard, the whole oven will be disguised with soil over the top and as the oven door is facing away from the fire, we hope that the bailiffs will not notice it. The only thing that will be visible is the chimney, made out of two tin cans. It should work, and I have asked that I am kept informed as to its viability.

I also left work on the oven when I heard that a young woman has been knocked down by a police horse and has a suspected fractured skull. This took place on the road near Southampton Village. There were a lot of concerned women around, and a couple were haranguing three mounted policemen, including, I believe, the one who had knocked the woman down with his horse at a canter. I was glad to see that Di was there, helping and going in the ambulance with the woman. I left her to deal with things, and gave her some money for phone calls, etc. She had the woman's backpack, as she appeared to be on her own and was foreign. She looked very pale and unhappy as she was lifted into the ambulance. I do hope she is all right.

The police have been a very mixed bunch. Personally, I have been treated well by them. Whether this is because of my grey hair and middle class accent, I don't know. Without doubt, there has been some violence, and in Britain if you are punk, or black or do not fit the respectability image, treatment is worse. Sad and wrong, but this is an unpleasant fact.

It was time to say goodbyes. My gear was in the car, plus a load of Ellie's, Christine's, Hil's, Hilary and Liz's and I was taking Ellie & Christine back to London. My passengers wanted to leave at 6 o'clock, so I gave myself an hour to go round the camp area. Some of the women were still dressed up and had painted faces, like Liz from Wales and Juley but the ones I may never see again like Ruth and Sally, were quiet and subdued and took some finding. All day they had been saying farewells to women, and although I felt like having a good cry, I knew it would make it harder for us all. Everyone wished me well in my new life as a student at Sussex, and masses of women said that they would be back at Orange Gate for the weekend of 3rd, 4th November when we would have a party for all those in court on the 5th. I am just wondering if I can keep away until then.

5th October 1984

I decided some time ago that the 10 Million Women for 10 Days would be the end of my journal for the year at Orange Gate at Greenham Common. Well it is over, finished, and now I must try to sum up my feelings about these last twelve months. It will not stop me writing more in the future, but this is somehow the end of an era.

Oddly enough, it ends as it starts with the inevitability of changing relationships. When I went to Orange Gate a year ago, I was in a state of personal crisis and unhappiness, trying to regain something that was irretrievably lost. I knew this, and that there is no going back in life. Whatever mistakes have been made, whether they are our own faults, or not, we must go on. The women, my friends, gave me this help, through their love and companionship. I became one of then, a Greenham woman. I was accepted, welcomes, wanted, needed, and out differences of age, background, country of origin in some cases, were unimportant. I was me, a woman, Ginette. Each time I arrived, I was always scared at that last bend in the road, that they would not be there, or they would be strangers, but never have I been disappointed. Always it was a coming home ceremony, not just to catch up on news of what had been happening, but a warmth and giving of pleasure on both sides. I am certain at times they must get sick to death of me talking too much, too loudly, standing on my head, particularly when drunk, and being obstreperous generally, but I am always welcomed.

I have learnt so much from these women. How to live in a commune, be strong, share, give, and wash in a kettleful of water. How to sleep outside in rain and frost, question authority on its stupidity, hate hierarchy. How to hug and show affection, naturally and without embarrassment. How not to not be afraid of what others think if I do not feel the time is right for me to do something even when others do. How to shit in a shit pit, and how to dig one. How to support and trust those with me, however hard the circumstances. Also, *how to have one hell of a good time!*

I take it as a real compliment when I am told that although most of these women are young enough to be my daughters, I am no older in my attitude and behaviour, we are all equal. Many young women wish their mothers had fought for their freedom the way I have and want me to meet and persuade them that anything is possible. We advise each other on problems and teenagers and sixty year olds have just as much to offer. I think and hope we have learnt from each other. Of course, I get on with some of the women better than I do with others, but the act of living in harsh conditions gives us a mutual respect for each other. Some may be better at washing up and others braver in times of adversity. There are verbal slanging matches, but it is better to have differences out in the open, although this is something that personally I am very bad at doing. There may be tears, shouting, but it usually ends with the antagonists hugging each other.

The main brickbat hurled at Greenham women are about the lesbianism, that no men are allowed there, and so family lives are broken up. First, it is women's space. We all know that if men were here, just living or being involved in actions, the whole concept of the place would change. We feel safe here without men. I think that if men did live here, without doubt, there would be hierarchy and roles to play, and during actions, violence would inevitably creep in however careful we all tried to be. Violence among women is much more likely to be verbal and tearful, rather than physical, although during big demonstrations when the fence is pulled there is a feeling of violence and power, which is not usually around and can therefore be frightening. If a woman is roughly treated by the police, women will yell both at the policeman and in support of the woman, but they will not use their fists or boots. I think most men would if pushed far enough. Next, lesbianism and home breaking. Yes, many of the women are lesbians, but there are also many heterosexuals. We are all just women; *so what*? It is far more the thought that we can manage at Greenham without men that worries many men. We have learned to be strong and self-sufficient and help each other, and close relationships are often formed. Some women become lesbians when they have lived there for a while, but I think this is because away from a place like Greenham it is hard to admit to being *'different'* or put a label on oneself. Here there is no normal or abnormal. We are here because we want to be, and if a friendship develops into love, it is expressed without fear or ridicule. It is all very natural and simple and beautiful. As in the outside world, some relationships last and are permanent, others transitory. Sometimes women get hurt but this is a real world and changes happen, however hard it may be. But, the overall help and understanding and talking it all through with women does help to relieve the pain of a lost love. Many women come here because they have already acknowledged that they are lesbians and are freer to express themselves with like-minded women. I think that the *'broken homes'* syndrome, which is often bandied about, would have happened whether the individual woman has or hasn't come to Greenham. It might be accelerated because there is space and time to sort problems and feelings out, but what will be is inevitable.

I originally came to Greenham on a CND ticket. I still believe completely and utterly that nuclear missiles are the most disastrous things the world has ever devised, but after a year of actions and living with women in peace and harmony, I think we can change the world and make it beautiful.

2nd – 5th November 1984

I could not leave the University until after my critical reading seminar, so I rushed to the car with clothes, sleeping bag etc., and piled them on top of the firewood I had collected from the woods at seven o'clock that morning. I was picking Hil up at Victoria coach station at 12.45, but I was about an hour late as the traffic was appalling. She had met up with my son Mark and we all had a drink and a sandwich, and Mark gave me £20 as I was the student now, and Hil and I left (plus my parking ticket) to go to Orange Gate. The rain bucketed down and it was a foul drive but the welcome was as warm as ever. Rebekah, Reading Anne, Jane, Judy, Annie back from her couple of weeks grape picking in France. Maureen, Jay and Faversham Hilary (who is now called 'Ary' to differentiate her from Deal Hil), Jill, Art school Julie, Rugby Julie who now lives at Red Gate, Karen, Fiona and other from the London Hospital, American Liz, Welsh Liz, Penni with flu, Val, Sarah and Jan from Kent with Blue, Isia, Jo, Helen and Listy. Over the weekend, Canterbury Liz with Karin and a school friend, Steph, tall Sue, Merseyside Karen, Abergavenny Anne, Waffle woman Jan, big Liz etc. It was a hell of a good weekend for meeting friends. There were so many women there that we had four fires going. I missed seeing Sally and Ruth, who had both gone home.

Hil and I got there just in time for supper, which was well up to standard, and of course, the wine and beer were produced quickly. The rain had eased by this time, although the ground was sopping wet and there was a rather cold wind. Most women slept in tents or simple single sheet benders. Hil and I opted for the car, which was warm even though the condensation dripped on our heads at times. We sat and talked for hours, exchanging news. I was very sad to hear that the oven had been firmly evicted, but at least it was used a few times, and a cake had been baked in it. We know that the principle works, and perhaps will make another one sometime. The evictions have been quite fierce and many things are missing. The bathroom went very quickly indeed, but now we have two kitchen prams rather than one. I think that most of the cooking and eating utensils are still around. The brown van is more crowded than ever, as Reading Ann's car, Mabel, needs something like £500 spending on her bodywork before she will pass her MOT, and nobody has that sort of money. I heard a nice story about Amelia, the car from the north side. Poor Amelia got really sick. In fact, let us be honest, she died of a big end going. Well she sat around at Red Gate and Sharples the bailiff kept on threatening to put her in the pound unless she was moved. He had no idea that the women were quite happy that she (Amelia) would be towed away as it would save them the expense, but they kept begging Sharples not to impound her. In the end, he said he was going to tow her away the next day. That night the women carefully unscrewed all the wheel nuts, and then adjusted them so they stayed in place. Along came Sharples in the morning, put a towrope on Amelia (which promptly broke), put a better one on, started pulling and all four wheels fell off at the same moment! He was furious as you can imagine, but it appears that later on he did see the joke, and did admit he really had been caught by the women on that occasion.

Eventually, we staggered off to our various beds at some time after midnight. Luckily, there was a night watch and I slept soundly. Even better, it was nice morning. After juice and coffee, I felt it was time for a blewit (mushroom) hunt. About half a dozen of us wandered off. Well, we walked a hell of a long way, found hundreds of marvellous fungi of all various, but I really was not sure if they were edible or not as I had no book with me. We did fine some blewits, so we had fried eggs, blewits and toast for breakfast, at lunchtime. Lots of women tried them, but only Jane decided that she really did not like them. Julie and Meryl then appeared and wanted to know if I was going to go round the gates in my car so Jane came with us, and we set off. At Yellow, we picked up Barbara who said she was in a cosmic state and out of the world (or she had a hangover). I also saw Rebecca J, with her bandaged hand that had been hurt inside the base a couple of nights previously. She and another woman went in, and climbed into a vehicle. A soldier got so incensed he smashed the windscreen with his rifle butt. It appears that the car was loaded with weapons. They were lucky not be badly hurt.

The five of us went on to Green, then Blue, then on to Red, as Julie had a fungi book and we wanted to walk in the nature reserve nearby and see what we could find and identify. It was beautiful there, quiet and peaceful, but there were so many different varieties of fungi; we could only identify a few before it started to get dusky and cold. Jane and I left the others and went via Thatcham *'offie'* and telephone, then back to Orange. I am not quite sure how it happened but once again, I managed to miss supper by going from one campfire to another, always getting there just after they'd eaten, so ended up with toast, eggs and more blewits for supper. At least I have proved that they are not poisonous to everyone's satisfaction!

At one of the fires, we discussed the women's actions during the ten days, and how we felt about things, and what we wanted to do in the future. One woman felt we ought to set up a sort of workshop in a Newbury home to learn skills from each other, and perhaps make things to sell. Then the usual money question came up. Commercialisation, problems of when we have money, and when we don't, etc. Oh, *for the ideal world without money.* This is one of the reasons why I am not sure whether Greenham is the real world. It is about the only place that I know of where you can talk like this without being thought a total loony.

I knew that Saturday night was going to be an active night inside the base. I am not nearly as brave as some of the women. I cannot face more than one charge at a time so I did not want to be involved. Keeping an eye on things from inside my sleeping bag in the car is the right way to operate in comfort! During the evening, some women quietly disappeared. This was going to be a big action. One of my tasks was to drive a woman down to the phone box sometime after midnight and alert the media as to what was going on. This we did, and perhaps because of this I missed our hospital women's firework display, although sometime during the evening I did hear the odd spluttering firework noise. Karen told me that most of the rockets, including the one with a label on saying '*Ginette is innocent*', slightly misfired (She said this the next day with a strained look on her face and a glass of Alka-Seltzer and brandy in her hand.) It was a nice idea anyway. Eventually, at about 1.30am, when the last '*merry*' woman had gone her way, I went to bed. It was a chilly night, and I was rather concerned when I woke briefly at about 6am and found that Hil was still not back. It sounds rather mean to say that it did not stop me sleeping for a couple more hours, when Helen, Jan and Blue returned. It was not until 9.30 that the others turned up.

The whole action had been well planned and executed. Women had previously checked the American buses parked inside the base and decided that the ignition key was very simple, and even a screwdriver would have worked. One woman had a suitable key that she brought. Three groups of ten cut their way at different places into the base, to meet up at the bus. Unfortunately, one group "*missed the bus*", and got there too late. The other twenty arrived, climbed into the bus, switched on the engine, drove across the base, past MoD cops, and arrived at the inner silo fence. They piled out, watched by a terrified little soldier in glasses, who shrieked into his walkie-talkie that there were women everywhere getting out of a bus. The women went over to the fence, and took turns in cutting. They did a lot of damage before they were arrested and put into the vans. It appears they were in quite a lot of personal danger as all the Americans in the vicinity had weapons, which they were waving about in a rather dangerous way.

The woman were taken to Newbury Nick, questioned and then left in the vans, where they spent a very cold night. In fact, the MoD cops were so concerned that they went back to the base and got urns of tea and coffee for the women. As usual, the arrests were arbitrary. Three of the women were accused of actual cutting. Two of these (both wearing leather jackets) had not even touched a pair of bolt cutters. The third had just had the cutters passed to her and was poised for cutting, but had not actually started. All of the twenty women will be pleading *not guilty* to the charges of attempted theft or collusion, because they allowed themselves to be driven in a stolen vehicle, although of course, it never went outside the base. Anyway, this charge means that they can make sure that they appear at the Crown Court, rather than magistrates, and there will be more publicity. Incidentally, the media (well the Guardian and the BBC news) featured the incident quite well. Apart from anything else, it shows up the total lack of co-operation between the Americans and British inside the base.

After breakfast Hil and Canterbury Liz were feeling quite tired having been awake all night, so the three of us went for a walk on the common. We found a nice warm place, an abandoned garden I think, with a park bench in the sunshine. Although it is November, we all pulled off sweaters and jackets. Hil and Liz fell asleep on the ground, and I went back to Orange. Jay, Ary and Sarah were going down to Eileen's to help her move a straw stack on to some palettes, so I joined them and spent a good afternoon heaving bales of straw about. I really enjoyed it, with cups of coffee, dogs, cats, a parrot, horses, cows and guinea fowl around. Anyway, Eileen is so supportive; it is good to give a bit of help occasionally.

I am not sure how it happened (again) but I still did not get to bed very early on Sunday night. I think it is the booze and the talk and company. You can put these in any order, but they do make

Greenham what it is. A lot of women had to leave, to go back to work or their other lives. Big Liz drove her fellow students back to their peace studies in Bradford, and many went off to Wales and London. Canterbury Liz and hospital Karen were amazing, they offered to do night watch, and started by clearing up the mayhem of dirty plates and general dishes left by the rest of us. Apart from anything else, I do remember being woken by the noise of someone making awful noises on a duck decoy whistle, not far from me. The noises stopped abruptly and it appears that Karen had gone over to the gate and told the man who was playing the whistle that if he did not stop, she would inform her MP that he was disturbing the peace! Greenham Peace Camp is full of amazing women.

Monday dawned bright and clear. Actually, it was grey and cool, but when Karen brought Hil and me a coffee in the car, it was bright, clear, and happy. I dressed really formally and respectably in my new (nearly new, bought in Sussex University market) Corduroy dungarees, clean shirt and knickers ready for court. I must confess that I had not washed underneath all these clean clothes since Thursday, as it had been rather too cold to strip down. At least I looked the part, with brushed hair and clean teeth. Mind you, after heaving straw around and living at Orange Gate, my hands and nails were not in the best shape, and the smell of wood smoke was, I think, was probably slightly strong.

I took Reading Anne, who was up in that ridiculous charge of cutting down a tree on the common, and Helen and Hil, with all their gear, as I'd offered to give them a lift near London We had no idea how long the court pleas would be. I was feeling slightly apprehensive as none of the women I had been charged with had been around at Greenham, but as soon as we arrived at the court, I saw Merseyside Karen. She told me she was going to plead guilty, but refuse to pay the fine, and so be sent straight to Holloway. She is trying to get a job and therefore does not want this case to hang around. Steph, tall Sue (who was arrested at a 12 noon blockade at Indigo the same day as I was) and lots of other women all decided we would please Not Guilty, come back on the 9th Jan as directed, then refuse to pay the fine and do our bit of porridge probably in Holloway. As the 9th Jan is a Wednesday, we think that we will be given not more than a week inside without remission. They do not let you out over the weekend, so we will just have the rest of

Wednesday, all day Thursday and then be let out on the Friday evening. I hope.

Many of the women did not turn up, and as it was only a day to give pleas, the whole affair was over for everyone by about 11.30. I was one of the last. I was called into court, Steph going out as I went in. She informed me that they were all very rude, but perhaps because she said this in a very loud voice, they were polite to me. I was directed to the dock. The chief magistrate read out my name, and the charge. I was asked how I was pleading. I said *"Not Guilty"* and I was informed that I would have to be back on the 9th January at 10am and I must be there as I would receive no further communication about this, and I was given unconditional bail. I just walked out. All too easy, really. Let us wait and see what happens next.

Anne, Helen and I decided to go back to Orange. On the way, we stopped for a chat at Red, then spent most of the rest of the day at Orange, saying goodbye all over again, and eating more breakfasts/lunches. Liz took Hil back to Canterbury as she had room in her car. At about 3pm Helen, Reading Anne and I left, to the strains of a woman with green hair playing her trombone for us. It had been another good time at Greenham, but by the time I had got lost a few times on my way to pick Ellie up in Surbiton from work, driven to Brighton, had a necessary bath, a meal and mulled wine, walked miles in Lewes to see the firework display and bonfire, I was quite weary. As I watched the vast bonfire burning, I did think the Greenham women could have done with some of the wood. I hope they are managing and the evictions, which came on Monday, were not too bad. All that work that Maureen did, tidying the van and clearing up will make things easier for those few left behind. I will be back soon. Work does rather get in the way.

16th – 17th November 1984

Annie, American Liz, Val, Alison and Judy. Pouring with rain. Val was ill, so we all went to the hospital in Basingstoke with her. More women arrived that night. Hil and her children in the Peace Van, Isia, Jan, Jill, Listy, etc., etc.

Saturday, went round to Yellow and talked to Sarah Hibbertson and others, then I went round to Green. CND and peace groups were giving out free food, four times a week. Women were being evicted five times a week, at least. Morale is still pretty good, but the wet is depressing. There are currently no camps at Indigo or Red. Everything has been cut down to minimum. Women still going inside. There was one nice story about fog, one really bad night. Annie went up to the Orange Gate where there was a young soldier on his own. She said hello to him. He asked her if she had seen a film called *"Fog"*. She said no, and asked him if he wished he *hadn't* seen it. He said, "Yes".

January 8th – 11th 1985

I realise in retrospect that I have been pretty scared at the unnerving prospect of time in Holloway. I think it was mainly the feeling of having no control over my own destiny for even a short while, and that it was the sort of situation that I no idea how I would react. It was all very well for the other Greenham women to tell me that it would be fine, and I've seen enough documentaries on telly about prison, not to make a real fool of myself by yelling 'let me out', but all the same I'm really glad it is all over. Whether its release of tension, coincidence or psychosomatic, I do not know, except that the night after I was released I was violently sick (a *very* rare thing for me) and then I developed an abscess on a tooth!

My preparations were careful. I left my car at Worthing, and having carefully packed a small bag with a change of clothes and books, I took a train then a coach to Thatcham. I reached Orange Gate having walked from the coach stop through the snow at about 7.30. By the time I arrived, I was boiling hot, and I kept a bit back from the blazing fire until I had cooled off. There was no mud this time, just ice and snow. The brown van, Petal from Red Gate, Tim, and of the course the women. Julie, Maureen, Jan the waffle woman, Maggie and a newcomer. Jan found some supper for me and we sat and talked. There was only one *'wind tunnel'* bender up near the fire (Julie still had one hidden), so Jan and the new woman decided to sleep in the van, and I offered to do a chunk of night watch, then take over from Maggie, in the bender with Maureen. It worked out well. At 3am, I kept falling asleep on the chair, as I was so tired. I then crawled into Maggie's sleeping bag, which was warm. Earlier we had had some trouble in de-freezing the water in the hotties, which had been shoved into the brown van for that morning's eviction. A frozen stiff right-angled hot water bottle is quite a funny sight. Anyway, I slept soundly until about 8am, then Maureen got up and brought me a welcome cup of coffee in bed. She and Jan decided to drive me to court and support me there, which was really encouraging of them.

Outside the courtroom, we met up with Steph, tall Sue, Lizzie, and others on trial and supporters. As usual, we all went and had a wash and brush up in the toilet, then sat and waited. And waited. Apart from waiting for other people to be tried, we discovered that Sue and Lizzie were going to be heard together, even though they had not even seen each other until they were put in the police van and had been arrested. They protested, and Sue was tried first. She was found guilty, refused to pay and was sent to Holloway for 7 days.

When we had first arrived Steph had anticipated in just paying her fine and going home, but then she was determined to stay. Her grown up daughter was with her and agreed that she would look after things back at home. Steph and I agreed to be tried together. However, before we went into the court, another woman was tried and found not guilty on various technical grounds. It was not until 1pm that we were eventually called. The magistrates consisted of one man and two women. We were told the procedure by the clerk of the court, what we could do and say, and then the prosecution called the arresting police officers.

Steph was dealt with first, but the police evidence was duplicated almost word for word. She maintained that she had not been arrested by the officer who claimed he had. I protested that I had only arrived at the scene of the blockade halfway through the statement that he made, and I had not been warned that if I sat down again I would be arrested. The chief magistrate asked the policeman if he had recognised me amongst the women who had been warned. He said that he could not remember, but I was certainly there when he arrested me! I had to agree with him on that point. Everyone fell about laughing.

Order was restored. Steph was asked if she wanted to go into the stand and make a statement. She said she would, then proceeded to give a most moving account of why she was there, because of her children, and the cost of armaments while so many starved in the world and the horror of nuclear weapons. I would not try to reproduce her actual words, but the Greenham women listening were all reduced to tears.

I had to follow that. All I managed to say was that I totally agreed with Steph, that most of my life I had been a law-abiding citizen, and if the American base with cruise missiles were not at Greenham, I would never have been arrested.

The magistrates went out to deliberate, and we waited for a while. They came back and said they found us guilty, and we would have to pay £25 plus £10 costs. We both refused to do so, so they said we would be sentenced to seven days in prison. The Greenham women all rushed up to wish us well, and we were led away. The first of the clanging and locking of doors until Friday morning.

We had to empty out our pockets, and be searched. Our possessions were taken from us, various forms were filled in, and I found myself back in Newbury nick, with the wooden bench, glass brick window, bare walls and floor. Well, I sat and waited. After an hour or so (my watch has been taken from me) a copper brought in a toasted cheese sandwich, bar of chocolate and small carton of Ribena, sent in by the Greenham women who realised we had missed lunch and so would be pretty hungry. It was welcome, as much for the concern from friends as the actual food.

It was getting dark by the time we were let out. We realised, as there were only three of us, the others must have got off. We would stick together, as much as we could, for the next few days. I should mention that in my cell there were various messages from Greenham women from most of the gates except Orange. I could not let that pass, so found a couple of dead matches on the floor and wrote "Orange Gate" and "♀♀" on the wall. It will probably be cleaned off soon enough, but it made me feel better. Writing graffiti can work.

We were locked in the back of a police transit van, and very cold it was too. Our possessions were in the front, so there was still no chance of a cigarette, but at least we could talk together. A policeman drove and a woman sat with him. I am not sure what time we got to Holloway, about 7 o'clock, I think. The entrance was formidable, and although there was tremendous relief to have the court case over and done with, at that moment, the last thing I wanted was to go behind those gates. Actually, it is not just one set of gates, but at least two or even three. It is hard to remember in detail, except that having driven in; the engine had to be switched off, the gate behind closed, then the one in front opened. We got out of the van, and were then officially handed over to Holloway prison.

The reception area had a lot of screws wandering about. Our possessions were put in front of us, we were asked if they were ours, and we were told to go along to a cubicle, undress and put on a dressing gown. Then back to the reception area with tables and chairs, and other waiting women in dressing gowns. Many of these were on remand with their trials actually on going, or were just arrested and were not granted bail. Some pretty foul food was produced, which we picked at, and then we were processed one by one. This consisted of having our possessions checked, and those we were not allowed to have with us, being placed in a sealed bag. For example, I had the choice of a packet of cigarettes or loose tobacco and paper for rolling. I had one tee shirt too many and I had to take off my Greenham Bracelet, and anklet. No toothpaste was allowed, only a toothbrush and a flannel. It all seemed rather arbitrary to me, but later I understood more. (Other things rather than toothpaste can be concealed in a tube.)

We were weighed, asked about past illnesses and whether we were vegetarians. We had to drop our dressing gowns to make sure we had nothing concealed on our bodies. We were given tooth powder and a sanitary towel bag, a bag of horrible soap, a towel, two sheets and a pillowcase. We were told to have a bath. There was plenty of hot water, but the bath was very tide-marked. We got dressed back into our own clothes. We were then escorted, by a screw with clanking keys, to our cells for the night.

The other inmates in the reception area were interesting. Questions were asked as to what women were *'in'* for. We all said *"Greenham"*, and we didn't have to explain further. We were accepted. Some of the women were subdued, others talkative. It seemed to me that most were in there for fairly pretty crimes.

There was one really quiet young woman who said nothing. She was tiny. She did not even come up to my shoulder. When asked why she was there, she said, "GBH" and we all fell about laughing. She then explained she had stuck a knife in a fellow's eye, and it had damaged it so badly he had the eye removed and now he had a glass one in its place. We all wondered how she had managed to reach that high. He was either minute, lying down, or she stood on a box to do it!

A young black woman was in for theft, and Shelly for a variety of petty cheque card forgeries and thefts, others for drug offences. We were a mixed bunch, but already I felt it was very much it was *'us against them.'*

Quite by chance tall Sue and I were put in a cell for four with Shelly. There was a young woman in there already. Steph had been rather a long time over her bath, so ended up in a cell on her own. My cell looked a bit like a hospital ward. Just inside the door, there was a washbasin and sink on one side. On the other, a lavatory with wall and door round it. The room was steaming hot, and we each grabbed a bed and dumped our stuff on it. The windows were long and narrow with opening sections. Each section was about eight inches wide, and in this particular cell it was impossible to see out, as behind was an opaque plastic screen. All I could see was a couple of square feet of frozen ground, and the same amount of sky. I instantly felt deprived of a visual perception. The door was notable. It was a double door, only one-half being opened. This had a covered hatchway in it, just large enough to pass food and mugs of tea through, and the other part had a thick glass slit in it at eye level, about 3 inches wide and fifteen inches long. There is never any real privacy. Each bed had a bell beside it, only to be used in times of real emergency we were told, and a socket for a radio, as in hospitals. However, there were no radios. In the other cell I was in, there were curtains, which could be pulled round each individual bed, but there were severe reprimands if an inmate did have the audacity to do so. The floor was lino and the walls painted pale green. To a prison visitor the impression would be of a pleasant room with pleasant décor, privacy, radio, etc. As an inmate, you don't see things the same way. I was far more conscious of the clanking doors, jangling keys, strident authoritative voices, petty rules which were often altered by individual screws, terrible stodgy food, tea and ever more tea (which I personally loathe), plastic utensils, and of course the continual feeling of being harassed and put down by those in command. The only chairs to sit on were hard and uncomfortable, so all the inmates either sit or lie on their beds all day. Each woman had a tiny wardrobe for clothes and a table. For a few days, I felt I could cope without problems. When I heard the stories of other women who were sentenced to this sort of life for years, I do not know how they could contemplate it so calmly.

The fourth woman in our cell introduced herself. Her name was Grace, and she was from Holland. She had been in Holloway on remand for seven months. She and a friend came to Britain for a holiday. At Dover their car was stopped by sniffer dogs and 6 ½ kilos of heroin were found hidden in it. She said she had no idea that it was there, and is certain it was put in the car by her stepfather who is in prison in Holland for drug running. The women I talked to all believed her story that she had been set up by him, and there was someone in the UK who would have stripped the car. She obviously has not had bail and she is separated from her friend who is in a different wing, so there is no 'association'. Her trial was meant to start a couple of weeks previously, but the prosecution asked for extra time, as they did not have their case ready. Grace is moved from wing to wing as the authorities want. In this particular reception wing, here is no work for her, so she just lies on her bed. She is twenty years old. Her English is good, but she finds it hard to read books in this language. It is much too far and expensive for friends to visit her. She receives mail, but finds this upsetting. The maximum sentence for drug pushing in this country is life, which means fifteen years. I may be a gullible fool, but I think she was framed and is innocent. Sue and I asked if we could contact anyone for her when we got out, but she just shrugged, thanked us and said no could help her. She just wants to know that her trial will be soon, and what her sentence will be. She had almost no hope that she will be found innocent.

Shelly was quite different: nervous, blond, restless & twenty. We asked her what she was in for. She started by saying that she was a naughty girl. She had done a bit of forgery on cheque cards and a bit of thieving, and she told us a story about how she and her fifteen year old sister had gone out and got drunk, and found a taxi with a Pakistani driver to get them home. On the way, they got him to stop at a kebab place, ordered some food and asked the driver to lend them some money, which they would pay back to him back when they got home. He did so, but a couple of streets from their home, they jumped out of the taxi and rushed off in different directions. The police caught them next day. Although she had lied, this was one of the charges. She had been to court that day, and thought she had to go back the next, but I think she had it muddled up. I did not like her story all that much, but then she started talking about her home, and that was she was worried about her mum, who was paralysed. This mum was only a couple of years older than I am. The paralysis was mainly caused by her *old man* regularly beating her since they were married. Shelly was also worried about her sister's child whom she was looking after. She thought the child would be put into care, and hoped someone would contact her sister in Scotland so she could look after the baby herself. Poor Shelly, she took the troubles of her family on her shoulders, and then could not cope herself.

Shelly could not settle. Sue and I got out our books and started to read, and Grace was lying quietly on her bed, thinking. Shelly asked what books we had. Sue had some heavy feminist books, and I had Tristram Shandy, Moby Dick and some Yeats poetry, which I am studying at University. Shelly had a look at the Yeats and said she had liked poetry at school. She glanced through it and said they did not look very easy or romantic, so I read her *The Lake Isle of Innisfree*.

She thought it was a lovely and went to the loo, tore off some paper and asked if she could copy out some other poems. She was a long time lying very quietly, and said she had remembered a poem she had written at school, which had won a prize. She recited it to us. It was all about an angel telling her to love someone faithfully. She is not stupid or bad, but will drift into more crime without help. Prison will keep her off the streets; teach her about more serious crime and drugs. It is not the answer to her problems.

At about 8.30, our hatch was opened and a screw said "Supper". This consisted of a mug of tea plus a large biscuit each. I took the tea and gave it to Shelly. I learnt quickly you never refuse *anything*, as someone else may like it even if you don't. At about 10.30 the corridor lights were turned out and a screw called to every cell, "*Goodnight, girls*" and as we were all tired, we washed, undressed and went to bed. I was surprised that there was no actual lights out time. We had individual very bright light over our beds, which we controlled ourselves. There was one central light, which had the switch outside the cell.

I was really tired, having been awake until 3 the previous night. Although the bed was very hard and the two radiators pumped heat into the room, I fell asleep quickly. The next thing I knew was the screw was shouting that it was time to get up and get breakfast.

When you are told to do something in prison, you do not hang around, but get a move on. We all washed and dressed and at about 7.45, our door was unlocked. We followed Grace to the eating area. We collected our mugs of tea, bowls of porridge if we wanted them, and two slices of white bread and one white roll with a knob of marge and a smear of dark jam. Prisoners have to provide their own sugar, but as you are not allowed to bring any in with you to reception, this is impossible to obtain, until you have been there long enough to earn money or get a visitor to send some in for you. We met up with Steph and with Georgina from Yellow Gate whose trial had been on Monday. She was having a lot of problems over food and drink as she is vegan, and the tea arrives in a huge pot with milk already added. In the end, she told us that she drank hot water, which she got from the kitchen. She was very concerned about the diet she as there was no fresh fruit or any of the supplements that she should have been receiving. Before we had half-finished our meal, the screws told us to hurry up and go back to our cells. We collected buckets and brooms on the way to scrub out.

We were locked inside, and cleaned. We should have scrubbed the floor, but did not worry as it was pretty clean. We then sat around on the beds, until two screws came and checked the room, we took the cleaning stuff away, then back again and the door was locked. Out of boredom, Shelly decided to wash her clothes. After a while a screw unlocked and told Shelly Sue and me that we were to go and see the assistant governor. More unlocking and locking. A crowd of us waited in an open area and once more, we were checked. In turn, we saw the AG. She told me that I should be released on the 13th but as that was a Sunday, I would get out on the 11th, which was the next day. She asked if I was going back to Newbury, and I said "no", as I had to go to Worthing to see my mother in the hospice. Reluctantly she said that she thought Worthing was about the same distance as Newbury, so I would be given a rail warrant there, plus a 60p fare to get to Victoria station.

I listened to other inmates talking about their home problems. One black woman, pregnant, and with a 2 and a 4 year old, was worried about getting the older child registered in the Catholic school near her home, rather than the ordinary primary, as there was a real violence problem in the playground here. The woman was in Holloway for ABH.

Back to our cells. Then a while later we are told to hurry up get our possessions together as we were moving to the discharge wing. We shoved our clothes and washing things into some very flimsy brown paper bags. We were told to wait by door that was unlocked, then locked behind us. Then, down corridors and upstairs. More locking and unlocking. Then we had to put our possessions on the floor in the eating area, and before were allocated a new cell. This time I was with Georgina and the other two women were already in the room, Blue and Sandra. The screws had to check that we had not acquired any possessions we should not have on the walk to this wing. We had to shed what we did not actually need for that night.

We were told to get our mug, knife, fork and spoon from the table in the cell, as it was lunchtime. I glanced at the clock: 11.15am. It was another Fawlty Towers type meal. The food consisted of grey potatoes, peas, carrots etc., all mushed up, and a few more bits of mushy veg under a cheese sauce. Plus, a bowl of, I think, apple tart, smothered in custard. It was stodgy and tasteless.

A visitor appeared with an AG so Georgina rushed to complain about the non-vegan food, and the rest of us picked at the least unpleasant bits on our plates. *Hurry, hurry, back to your* cells, must be locked in quickly. Before we go, we tip the uneaten food into a bucket and take the plates back to the kitchen, but we keep our mug, knife, fork and spoon.

After an hour or so, our door was unlocked and we had to go through our possessions in the eating area. I was allowed to keep a book with me, but it appears that this is arbitrary and very much depends on the individual screw. The rest of our things were put in paper bags with our names on them and stapled shut. Back to the cell to be locked in again. We talked for a while, then all dozed off, only to be awakened by the hatch in the door being opened and a screw shouting in "got any dinner plates in there?" What the hell would we want foul old plastic dinner plates in our rooms for at 3.30 in the afternoon? I think it was just to wake us up.

At 4.15 teatime, we collected mugs etc., only to receive a plate of pretty foul macaroni cheese (no good for Georgina), bread and butter and more tea. Eat up quickly, no time to finish the tea, take it back to the cell. Then the door was locked again. It remained that way until we were on our way to release, or to the courts at about 6.15 the next morning. It was a long time to be banged up, but quite normal according to the other women.

Sandra was thin, fair-haired, white faced, a junkie. Her street had been done over by the drug squad and now she was in Holloway. She was on remand and although she had been to the medical wing, she felt that they did not really help her and she hated it there, so she was suffering quite severe withdrawal symptoms. These consisted mainly of stomach and leg cramps, and not sleeping. She was very nervy and anxious. She said the drugs they found were mainly for her own use and that although she helped friends sometimes she was not a real pusher. She knew that a certain *'pink liquid'* type medicine (methadone) helped to relieve the cramp, but all she was given was an aspirin tablet to swallow. I think she had been in prison quite a few times before as she seemed knowledgeable about life inside, but she was not very forthcoming. She was in her mid-twenties.

Blue was the real extrovert. Rather dramatic looking with loose afro-style dark hair, and a completely transparent complexion, caused of course, by the drugs. She had been on remand in Holloway for a month and said it was amazing that now she could see the black pupils in her eye, the first time in years, and had started smoking pot when she was 12. She had been working as a secretary and her boss knew all about her addiction. She was very knowledgeable about prison, and the drug scene descriptions she gave were amazing. She had dealt in every know drug (except glue sniffing, which she thoroughly disapproved of!), had even taken magic mushrooms to Morocco, had grown about 150 cannabis plants in an attic, and traded and pushed everything. She swore that she had never sold drugs to kids, just to her own friends of her age. She told us about various bad trips she had had, but when I asked if she would kick the habit when she came out, she shrugged and said she would like to, but she had no other friends other than drug takers. I felt she was pretty high up the hierarchy scale inside Holloway.

Blue told us everything about Holloway. She said it was about the worst women's prison in the country, although at Durham they still had potties and *slop out*. She knew many of the women and spent quite a lot of time during the evening, calling to friends through the slitted window (this one had no opaque plastic outside so you could see into the exercise yard and a few other windows). This calling happens every night, although if a prisoner is found doing it, she loses privileges. The screws try to stop close friendships and lovers from seeing too much of each other, so they are put in different wings. So they can meet up, they all go to church every Sunday, even if they cannot actually talk. Once a woman is sentenced, she can go to educational classes and this is another way of meeting. Everything done there is to try to beat the system and the screws. The screws spend all their time trying to put you down in one way or another, and the inmates bounce back, or find a way round. Survival techniques abound. Anything that you want in prison can be got. Drugs for example. Wrapped in cling film, they can be stuck up your crutch, or swallowed. It appears that one woman was seem palming something into her mouth just before she got into Holloway, so was sent straight to the nurse who gave her medicine to make her vomit. She vomited through her fingers, using them as filters, and the drugs came into the prison. Another way is for packages to be chucked overt the wall into the exercise yard. They are picked up by the prisoners who sweep the yard, and shared between the sweeper and the inmate who is expecting it. If you have money and friends outside you are all right inside.

Apart from the wings with convicted inmates just doing their time, there are the medical and psychiatric units, and mother and child areas. The psychiatric prisoners are called the *"muppets"*, and some of them are just sad, and others violent. It sounded an unpleasant place. The general feeling was that women in there were not getting the sort of help they needed. Most addicts and junkies went to the medical wing when they first arrived, but got out as soon as they could. The mother and child was for women with babies, but I do not know much about it, except that women from other wings went there to help with the cleaning. Then of course, there was the punishment area. These were all single cells, cold and bare, no furniture. The offender was allowed to keep her clothes on these days, but just had one blanket. Food was passed to her on a tray, no plate, but all slopped together: meat, custard, potatoes, apple pie, gravy, etc. The punishment was usually for two or three days.

The stories of drugs and prisons happened on one side of the room, while Georgina and I told Greenham stories. Blue said that she had meant to come down and visit the women there. Perhaps when she finished her sentence she would come. As she had already told us that the law was heavy on pushers these days and that she could get fifteen years, we did say amongst laughter that we hoped we would not still be there. At the usual time, supper was brought to our hole in the door. A small cake for three of us and two water biscuits with a smear of jam for Georgina, and of course tea with milk in it. Blue, for health reasons could not drink unboiled milk, so the argument started. The screw said that 'no milk' was not down on Blue's form, so she had to have it with milk. Blue said surely they knew her well enough by now to know she never had had unboiled milk, and she had it put down on the form again this time. Anyway, what about Georgina? She managed to get plain hot water.

I waited, handed my mug up to the slot and said very politely, "coffee and milk, no sugar". For a moment there was a stunned silence, then the screw said, "We're clean out of coffee" and the tension went. But they did not get their tea, either.

I asked what the screws were like. The women resented a lot of them, said they made up the rules as they went along, or bent them in their own favour, so the inmates never really were sure if they were obeying them or not. They said some few were quite nice with a sense of humour, but some were really heavy. I must say, by the look of some, I would not care to get in their bad books. It appears when they first start they have a six-week probation period, when they watch what is going on, and then they get their uniform and are screws. There could be quite a lot more to it than that, that the inmates do not see, and I believe they have to have various tests before they are employed. However, I do not think the training is that arduous. I think that many of the male screws are ex-army or police, but I do not have any idea where the women come from.

We heard all about the Christmas riots. It was started mainly because of the bad food, lack of association and general discontent. It was not started at a very clever time, as the women were banged up, so they rioted in their individual cells. They broke the furniture and windows, burnt mattresses, and blockaded doors. It was complete mayhem in some wings. The authorities got very worried, and called in help from the men's prison, police and firemen. The place was swarming with men. The barricading of the doors was rather a failure, as the entire door can be lifted off its hinges from the outside, and the bits of furniture pushed up tight against it, more or less fall down. I do not think it did much good for the women, but at least they showed that they are capable of causing real trouble if they are pushed around too much.

I learnt that cigarette lighters were not allowed inside because of the fuel in them. Matches are always in short supply, and women split each in two, so they have enough. Photos are allowed, but not Polaroid ones. These, it appears, have acid on the back from when they are processed in the camera. I suppose some inmate must have made use of it sometime in the past, but I have no idea what for.

With all this talk going on I did not get much reading done. At about 10.30 we heard the screw walking down, calling out "*Good night, girls*" top each door. We looked at each other. We all hated being called girls, and when she came to our door, we waited, then called out: "*!!Women!!*" in unison, and listened. Down the rest of the corridor, she called out "*Goodnight*" only.

We had been warned we would have an early call in the morning and we must leave the place tidy, with fold blankets etc., and we must hurry up and be ready. Blue said there would be ages to wait, hanging around, so we knew what to expect. We got ready for bed, and I fell asleep quickly.

The next thing I knew was the central light being switched on and a strident voice telling up to get up. We did so, and were ready when the door was unlocked at 6.30. We met up with Steph and Sue clutching their possessions, and were then told to wait by a door. A screw, with a pile of files, unlocked the door for our group, and then locked it behind us. We went thought four more doors like that, were told to leave our things out in a passage, and go into room with tables and chairs and women milling about.

The ones on trial were a bit apprehensive, but those going out were really happy. Breakfast, consisting of a couple of bits of white bread and a lump of very greasy bacon was brought in, plus the usual mugs of tea. We sat and had some, but by now all I could think of was a cup of coffee. We hung round for about an hour talking and getting impatient. One woman who said she had not done much, just a bit of burglary and theft, and a very quiet Asian sat nearby looking frightened. A big black woman was getting her friends to put her turban on for her. I saw it being carefully wound round, and then taken off at least three times.

Blue and Sandra were called, so we said goodbye and wished them luck. Then it was my turn, first go into a cubicle get undressed, put on a dressing gown and wait. My clothes were searched (I'm not sure what they expected to find on me when I was going out of the place) and once more I had to drop the dressing gown and turn in a circle. Then back into my clothes, pick up my paper bags, go to a desk and be told that my £2.46 would be increased by 60p for the fare to Victoria. This would be given to me at the gate with my rail warrant. On to the next desk, where my things were checked and I was given back my holdall and other goods taken from me when I arrived. I had to stuff everything into my bag in a rush, and then we were led to the gate. It was nearly 8.30. I was asked my number, D23485, and name, given my warrant and money. The second gate was opened and I was free.

Georgina went off quickly to visit her daughter who lived nearby, and a friend of Sue's had driven from Wales to take her home, so Steph and I joined them in a coffee before we went our separate ways. The last we saw of some of our fellow inmates was an hour later when we were saying goodbye on the main road, and I saw a prison bus go past. There were a lot of men in it and a few women. I waved half-heartedly, checked and saw a mass of faces and wildly waving arms. We all waved like made as they went round a corner.

It is presumptuous of me to think I know all about Holloway after one evening, one day and two nights, but it certainly left a strong impression on me. Perhaps on a personal level I was relieved that as a Greenham woman on a piddling little charge, the other inmates did not think I was just playing at prison, they really seemed to respect and understand what we were doing. We were all there for a variety of reasons. Whatever these happened to be, they banged us up together, and we suffered the same humiliations and treatment.

One woman said that the Greenham inmates had helped to get better conditions as they knew who to complain to, and how to get things changed. For everyone inside, I think it is the general feeling of being put down, pushed around, treated like idiots, strongly pressurised all the time, and of course being locked in a cell for such long periods, which would become more and more galling. I am not sure after a period whether I would totally become a 'Yes, Miss' person, or fight like hell against the pricks. The continuous jangling of keys reminded me of my convent school where the nuns had long jingling rosaries hanging from their waists. I had no control over my life then, and in prison, I was a naughty child again, being dictated-to by those for whom I had no respect.

The argument about prison has been going on as long as crimes have been committed and people have been locked up. It does keep criminals off the streets for a while, but none of the women I saw in there would be deterred by a sentence. The young ones will learn new tricks from the old hands, and the old hands go back their previous life and friends. I know that the three of us who went in together certainly will not think twice about sitting down in the road in similar circumstances at Greenham in the future.

November 2014: Afterword

I was born Ginette Bell-Syer on the 26th May 1933 in Worthing to very conservative parents. I had one sister, Gina, who was five years older than me. Gina died in 2014, after a long and very sad illness. Our school was the local convent, which I left at 16; Gina went to live in Canada that same year. I did a secretarial course at Brighton Tech, worked locally for a while then moved to London. I met my husband John there, and became involved in CND and the Aldermaston marches. My son, Mark, was born in 1956 and we moved to Cambridge for five years. Then we moved to Deal, on the Kent coast for 25 years.

I have had many jobs, mostly part-time: with a pony breeder, as an assistant at a pottery, digging lugworms for fish bait, etc. In the 1970's & early 80's, with a friend, I assisted and co-wrote about 16 books and many articles ranging from cookery, country living, windmills, sailing & photography.

During this writing period, CND became a big part of my life. When a local group member died, and left some money, we purchased a camper van and painted *"Peter Darlington Peace Van"* on the side. Our group lent the vehicle to the Greenham Common women. We went to retrieve it in November 1982, when we were told the van was being evicted, the event that marks the start of this journal. As soon as I arrived at Greenham, I knew I that would be back again, to stay with the women. Even though it was chaotic, muddy & cold, I felt at home.

* * * * *

My time at Orange Gate at the age of 50 was remarkable: I had found myself at last. The Orange Gate Journal describes my frequent journeys and the happenings. Driving from East Kent through London (no M25 orbital motorway in the early nineteen eighties) became routine. The women of Greenham inspired me to change my life, go to university, to get divorced and become the real me, which I very happily did. An inheritance from my mother who died a few weeks after the end of the journal enabled me to buy a small flat in Brighton and get a clerical job. Later, I went on a trekking holiday to Nepal and moved in with a woman near Slough. On the strength of my degree, I got a good job with Social Services as a carer's worker. After six years, I returned to Brighton with a job supporting people with HIV/AIDS.

I retired when I was 67, and now live happily with my partner Millie in a bungalow. I am 81, and pretty fit, as I do gardening and walking on the South Downs with women from Brighton. I still keep in touch with Greenham friends and think of my time at Orange Gate with the wonderful women who gave me such support and happiness.

Ginette